English Vocabulary in Use

Elementary

SECOND
EDITION

with answers

Michael McCarthy
Felicity O'Dell

CAMBRIDGE
UNIVERSITY PRESS

CAMBRIDGE
UNIVERSITY PRESS

University Printing House, Cambridge CB2 8BS, United Kingdom

Cambridge University Press is part of the University of Cambridge.

It furthers the University's mission by disseminating knowledge in the pursuit of education, learning and research at the highest international levels of excellence.

www.cambridge.org
Information on this title: www.cambridge.org/9780521136174

© Cambridge University Press 2010

First published 2010
7th printing 2014

Printed in Dubai by Oriental Press

A catalogue record for this publication is available from the British Library

ISBN 978-0-521-13620-4 Edition with answers and CD-ROM
ISBN 978-0-521-13617-4 Edition with answers
ISBN 978-0-521-13619-8 Edition without answers
ISBN 978-0-521-13621-1 Test Your English Vocabulary in Use Elementary

Contents

Thanks and acknowledgements

A book like this owes a great deal to many people.

Many thanks are due to the editorial team under Nóirín Burke at Cambridge University Press who steered this book through the preparation of this new edition. We are particularly grateful to Caroline Thiriau, Hazel Meek, Emily Hird and Alison Silver, who have provided us at different stages of the process with generous help and guidance. Thanks are also due to Jeanette Alfoldi and the production team, and Lucy Mordini for the proofreading.

Our domestic partners as always get a special thank you for their tolerance and support. It is a great sadness that Vlad will not be able to enjoy seeing the final copies of a book that he did more to help produce than he could ever have realised.

We would also like to thank the teachers and students who participated in focus groups at the following institutions:

UK
Bell School, Cambridge
Cambridge Academy of English, Cambridge
Regent, London
Oxford College International, London

Belgium
UCL, Louvain-la-Neuve
ULB, Brussels
British Council, Brussels
University of Namur

Russia
Sodruzhestvo School, Moscow
EF language school, Zhulebino, Moscow
Moscow State University
BKC – International House (IH), Moscow

Michael McCarthy
Felicity O'Dell

Cambridge, September 2009

Development of this publication has made use of the Cambridge International Corpus (CIC). The CIC is a computer database of contemporary spoken and written English, which currently stands at over one billion words. It includes British English, American English and other varieties of English. It also includes the Cambridge Learner Corpus, developed in collaboration with the University of Cambridge ESOL Examinations. Cambridge University Press has built up the CIC to provide evidence about language use that helps to produce better language teaching materials.

Illustrations by: Amanda Macphail, Gary Wing, Gillian Martin, Humberto Blanco, Jo Taylor, Kathy Baxendale, Vicky Woodgate, Kate Charlesworth, Kathryn Baker, Mark Duffin

Introduction

To the student

This book will help you learn around 1,250 new words and phrases. You can use the book yourself, without a teacher. You can do the units in any order you like.

Here is what the pages look like:

The left-hand page presents the new vocabulary.

The left-hand page is divided into sections.

Error warnings and learning tips are also given on the left-hand page.

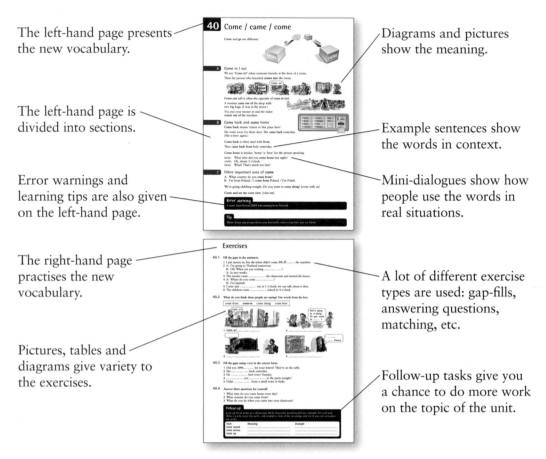

Diagrams and pictures show the meaning.

Example sentences show the words in context.

Mini-dialogues show how people use the words in real situations.

The right-hand page practises the new vocabulary.

A lot of different exercise types are used: gap-fills, answering questions, matching, etc.

Pictures, tables and diagrams give variety to the exercises.

Follow-up tasks give you a chance to do more work on the topic of the unit.

The Answer key at the end of the book is for you to check your answers to the exercises after you do them. The Answer key sometimes has more than one answer. This is because there is often not just one correct way of saying something. The Answer key also has possible answers for most of the exercises which are open-ended, or where you are asked to talk about yourself.

The Index at the end of the book has all the important words and phrases from the left-hand pages. The Index also tells you how to pronounce words. There is a list of phonemic symbols to help you understand the pronunciation on page 158.

It is a good idea to have a dictionary with you when you use the book so you can check the meaning of something, or translate a word into your own language. Sometimes, you will also need a dictionary for the exercises; we tell you when this is so. You also need a vocabulary notebook to write down new words. See page 172 for ideas on how to learn and remember these new words.

We hope you like this book. When you have finished all the units in this book, you can test yourself using the book of tests that accompanies this book, *Test Your Vocabulary in Use Elementary Second Edition*. Then you can go to the next book in the series, *English Vocabulary in Use: Pre-intermediate and intermediate*, and after that, to the higher levels, *English Vocabulary in Use: Upper-intermediate* and *English Vocabulary in Use: Advanced*.

To the teacher

This book can be used in class or as a self-study book. It is intended for learners at A1–A2 levels of the Council of Europe scale. It aims to take learners with a very basic level of vocabulary to a point where they can use approximately 2,000 words and phrases and teaches them around 1,250 new words and phrases. The vocabulary has been chosen for its usefulness in everyday situations, and we consulted a written and spoken corpus of present-day English to help us decide on the words and phrases to be included. The new vocabulary (on average 20–30 items per unit) is presented with illustrations and explanations on the left-hand page, and there are exercises and activities on the right-hand page. There is an Answer key and an Index with pronunciation for all the key vocabulary.

The book focuses not just on single words, but also on useful phrases and collocations. For example, difficult teaching points such as the difference between **do** and **make** are dealt with through collocation (we **do** our homework, but we **make** mistakes), and useful phrases (e.g. **come along**) are presented.

The book is organised around everyday topics, but also has units devoted to core verbs such as **get** and **bring / take**. Typical errors are indicated where appropriate, and the most typical meanings and uses are focused on for each key item. The units in the book can be used in any order you like, but it is often a good idea to do blocks of units based round the same topic (e.g. *People*, *At home*, *Leisure*).

The right-hand pages offer a variety of different types of activities, including traditional ones such as gap-filling, but also more open-ended ones and personalised activities which enable learners to talk about their own lives. Although the activities and exercises are designed for self-study, they can easily be adapted for pairwork, groupwork or whole-class activities in the usual ways. For example, where there are dialogues, students can take the speaking parts and practise the conversations, and where the exercises have questions and answers, students can practise asking each other the questions and answering them. See who has the best ideas for recording vocabulary in their notebook. The Answer key sometimes gives alternative answers to the exercises, and also gives possible model answers for the more personalised ones.

When the learners have worked through a group of units, it is a good idea to repeat some of the work (for example, the exercises) and to expand on the meaning and use of key words and phrases by extra discussion in class, and find other examples of the key items in other texts and situations. This can be done at intervals of one to three months after first working on a unit. This is important, since it is usually the case that learners need five to seven exposures to a word or phrase before they can really know it, and no single book can do enough to ensure that words are always learnt first time.

When your students have finished all the units in this book, they can test themselves using the book of tests that accompanies this book, *Test Your Vocabulary in Use Elementary Second Edition*. They will then be ready to move on to the next book in this series: *English Vocabulary in Use: Pre-intermediate and intermediate*, by Stuart Redman.

Find more resources for teachers at www.cambridge.org/elt/inuse

We hope you enjoy using the book.

1 The family

A Family words

A family tree for some of Anne and Ivan Sorokin's **relatives** or **relations**.

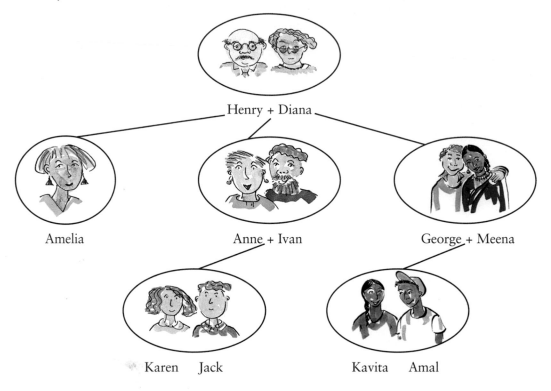

Henry + Diana

Amelia   Anne + Ivan   George + Meena

Karen   Jack   Kavita   Amal

Ivan and Anne and their **children**
  Ivan is Anne's **husband** and Karen and Jack's **father**.
  Anne is Ivan's **wife** and Karen and Jack's **mother**.
  Anne and Ivan are Karen and Jack's **parents**.
  Karen is Anne and Ivan's **daughter**. Jack is their **son**.
  Karen is Jack's **sister**. Jack is Karen's **brother**.

Henry and Diana
  Henry is Karen and Jack's **grandfather**. Diana is their **grandmother**.
  Henry and Diana are Karen and Jack's **grandparents**.
  Karen is their **granddaughter**. Jack is their **grandson**.

Amelia, George and Meena
  George is Karen and Jack's **uncle**.
  Amelia and Meena are Karen and Jack's **aunts**.
  Karen is Amelia, George and Meena's **niece**. Jack is their **nephew**.
  Kavita and Amal are Karen and Jack's **cousins**.

B Expressions

Have you got any brothers and sisters?   No, I am **an only child**.

Do you come from a big family?   Yes, I have three brothers and two sisters.

> ### Error warning
> We say 'my/his wife' (singular) but 'our/their wives' (plural).

Exercises

1.1   Look at the family tree on the opposite page. Complete the sentences.

1 Kavita is Amal's   *sister*
2 Amal is Kavita's   ....
3 Anne is Kavita's   ....
4 Ivan is Amal's   ....
5 Diana is Amal's   ....
6 Henry is Kavita's   ....
7 Amal is Ivan's   ....
8 Kavita is Ivan's   ....
9 Meena is Kavita's   ....
10 Meena is George's   ....
11 Karen is Amal's   ....

1.2   The Sorokins have some other relatives. Complete the sentences about them.

Sanjay   Alexander and Leila

Meena has a brother, Sanjay. Sanjay is Kavita and Amal's ¹*uncle* .... and Sanjay's wife is their ² .... Sanjay and his wife have one son, Prem. Prem is an ³ ....

Henry's parents are still alive. Alexander is Henry's ⁴ .... and his ⁵ .... Leila is Henry's ⁶ ....   Alexander and Leila have three ⁷ .... – Amelia, Ivan and George. Ivan and George and their ⁸ .... , Anne and Meena, love their ⁹ .... and visit them as often as possible.

1.3   Ask a friend these questions. Then write sentences about your friend and their family. For example, *Chen has one brother but no sisters.*

1 Have you got any brothers and sisters?
2 Have you got any cousins?
3 Have you got any nieces or nephews?
4 Have you got any grandparents?
5 Do you come from a big family?

1.4   Cover the opposite page. How many family words can you write down in two minutes? Check what you wrote carefully with the book. Did you spell everything correctly? Which words did you forget?

> **Follow-up**
>
> Draw your family tree. Then write sentences. Write about your relations. *Anne is my mother.* Use a dictionary to help you.

2 Birth, marriage and death

A Birth

Anna **had a baby** yesterday.

He **was born** at 1.15 yesterday morning.

He **weighed** 3 kilograms.

They are going to **call** him John – **after** John, his grandfather. His grandfather's **birthday** is June 16th too – but he was born in 1945!

The baby's parents **were born** in 1974.

Error warning

We say: Anna **had a baby** [NOT Anna ~~got a baby~~]. We say: He/She **was born** [NOT He/She ~~born~~ or He/She ~~is born~~].

B Marriage

If you do not have a partner, you are **single**.

If you have a husband or wife, you are **married**.

If your husband or wife dies, you are **widowed**.

If your marriage breaks up, you are **separated / divorced**. (the marriage has legally ended)

Bill and Sarah **got married**.

The **wedding**

bride

(bride) **groom**

Error warning

Sarah **got married** to Bill [NOT ~~with~~ Bill].

They **(got) married** in 1988. (*married* without *got* is more formal)

They went on their **honeymoon** to Italy.

They **were married** for 20 years.

C Death

Then Bill became **ill**.

He **died** last year.

He **died of** a heart attack.

Error warning

Bill is dead [NOT Bill ~~is died~~ or Bill ~~is death~~].

The **funeral**

Exercises

2.1 **Think of people you know. Where were they born? When?**

1 My mother was born in Scotland on July 4th 1957.
2 ....
3 ....
4 ....
5 ....

2.2 **Find a word on the opposite page which means …**

1 the name for a woman on her wedding day.   bride
2 the name for a man on his wedding day.
3 what you are if you haven't got a partner.
4 to be 57 kilograms.
5 what you are if your marriage has legally ended.
6 a religious service for a dead person.
7 a holiday after a wedding.
8 what you are if your husband or wife dies.

2.3 **Complete the sentences with words from the box.**

~~in~~	after	of	to	born	on

[1] In .... 2003 Anne got married [2] .... Robert Smith. Unfortunately, Robert's grandmother, Rosemary Smith, died [3] .... old age soon after their wedding. Robert and Anne were [4] .... their honeymoon when she died. Anne's baby daughter was [5] .... two years later. They called the baby Rosemary, [6] .... Robert's grandmother.

2.4 **When were these people born and when did they die? Write sentences.**

1 Genghis Khan (1162–1227) Genghis Khan was born in 1162 and died in 1227.
2 Christopher Columbus (1451–1506)
3 Leonardo da Vinci (1452–1519)
4 Princess Diana (1961–1997)
5 Heath Ledger (1979–2008)

2.5 **Complete the sentences using *died*, *dead* or *death*.**

1 Jill's grandfather died .... last year.
2 His .... made her very sad.
3 Her grandmother has been .... for five years now.
4 She .... of a heart attack.
5 Now all Jill's grandparents are ....

2.6 **Write about your family. Use words and expressions from the opposite page.**

Here are some ideas for making your sentences.

I have .... I/my .... got married in .... (year). For my/his/her honeymoon, I/he/she went to ....

I have / my .... has .... children. They were born in .... and .... (years).

3 Parts of the body

A Head and face

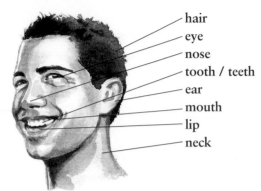

- hair
- eye
- nose
- tooth / teeth
- ear
- mouth
- lip
- neck

B Arm and leg

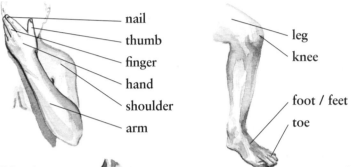

- nail
- thumb
- finger
- hand
- shoulder
- arm
- leg
- knee
- foot / feet
- toe

C Rest of body

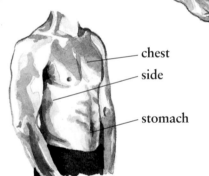

- chest
- side
- stomach

We have **skin** covering our bodies.

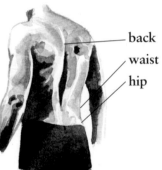

- back
- waist
- hip

D Inside the body

  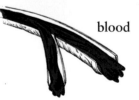

heart   brain   blood

E Pronunciation problems

eye /aɪ/   knee /niː/   stomach /ˈstʌmək/   heart /hɑːt/   blood /blʌd/   foot /fʊt/   tooth /tuːθ/

F Singular and plurals

one foot – two feet   one tooth – two teeth

Hair is a singular word. My hair is very long – I must cut it soon.

Error warning

Usually we use my, your, his, her, etc. with parts of the body. Jane is washing her hair [NOT Jane is washing the hair]. I have a pain in my leg [NOT I have a pain in the leg].

(See Unit 6: Health and illness.)

Exercises

3.1 Here are the names of some parts of the body with the letters mixed up. What are they?

1 eken   _knee_.....................   6 are   ....

2 osen   ....   7 hotot   ....

3 rathe   ....   8 buhtm   ....

4 hamcost   ....   9 akbc   ....

5 olderush   ....   10 tiwas   ....

3.2 Complete these sentences with words from the opposite page.

1 A hand has five ..._fingers_............ .

2 A foot has five ....

3 An adult has 32 ....

4 You smell with your ....

5 The .... is a symbol of love.

6 You hear with your ....

7 The child sat on her father's ....

8 Your .... type can be A, B, AB or O.

9 You think with your ....

3.3 Correct the mistakes in the sentences.

1 I have a pain in ~~the~~ side. _I have a pain in my side._

2 That woman has got very big foots.

3 My grandfather has a pain in the shoulder.

4 The baby has already got two tooths.

5 The little girl needs to wash the face and the hands before dinner.

6 My hairs are dirty. I need to wash them.

3.4 Parts of the body are often used in compound nouns too. Complete these nouns with a word from the opposite page.

1 ....._arm_....chair   3 ....stick   5 ....scarf

2 ....ball   4 ....brush   6 ....bag

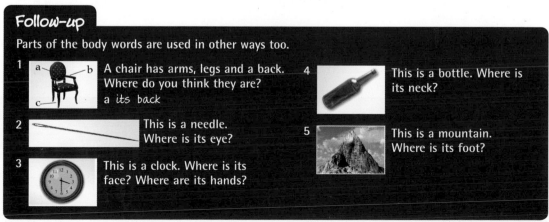

Follow-up

Parts of the body words are used in other ways too.

1   A chair has arms, legs and a back. Where do you think they are?
a _its back_

2   This is a needle. Where is its eye?

3   This is a clock. Where is its face? Where are its hands?

4   This is a bottle. Where is its neck?

5   This is a mountain. Where is its foot?

4 Clothes

A Clothes

hat coat jacket scarf gloves shoes trainers boots suit socks skirt tie T-shirt watch shirt dress ring belt sweater / jumper

B Plural words

These words are always plural in English. They need a plural verb.

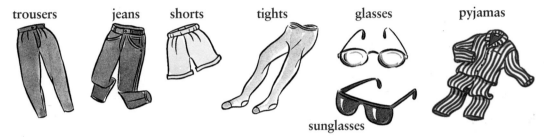

trousers jeans shorts tights glasses pyjamas sunglasses

My suit **is** new but these trousers **are** old. Her jeans / shorts / tights **are** blue.

Note: You say: **a pair of** trousers / shorts / glasses, etc.

Verbs

You **wear** clothes but you **carry** things.

You **wear** glasses.

Naomi **is wearing** a long red coat. She's **carrying** a suitcase and a small **handbag**.

You can also say: Naomi **has** (**got**) a red coat **on**.

You **carry** a **bag** and an **umbrella**.

In the morning you **get dressed** or **put** your clothes **on**. At night you **get undressed** or you **take** your clothes **off**.

> **Error warning**
> You put clothes on but you take clothes off [NOT ~~put clothes off~~].

> **Tip**
> When you get dressed in the morning, say to yourself *Now I'm putting on my socks. Now I'm putting on my shoes* and so on.

Exercises

4.1 Complete the sentences.

1 Joe has a job interview today, so he's wearing a smart su.it................... , a white sh.................... and a t.................... .
2 Julia's not working today, so she's wearing a T-.................... and sh....................s.
3 Liz is going to play tennis. She's wearing white s....................s and tr....................s.
4 Gianni is going to a business meeting. He's ....ing a b.................... with his papers and laptop.
5 My trousers are too big. I have to wear a b.................... .
6 It's cold today. I'll wear my j.................... , and I'll take my c.................... too.

4.2 Match the item of clothing with the part of the body.

| scarf | belt | shoe | hat | glove | glasses | tights | ~~ring~~ |

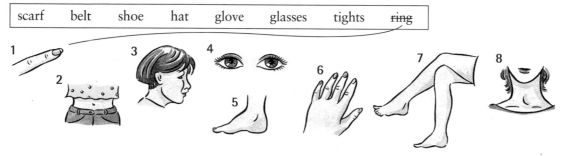

4.3 Complete the sentences with one of the verbs in the box and put it in the right form.

| be | wear | carry | have |

1 Nick's jeans are.................... blue and his T-shirt .... red.
2 Julia .... jeans and a T-shirt today.
3 Meena .... got a red coat on and she .... some flowers.
4 Sarah's dress .... old but her shoes .... new.
5 Last year Jim's trousers .... white. Now they .... grey.
6 .... this a new pair of jeans?
7 My favourite pyjamas .... dark green.
8 Kim .... a new pair of shorts.

4.4 Label the picture.

1 sunglasses
2
3
4
5
6
7
8
9
10

4.5 Complete the verbs in the table.

morning	night
get dressed....................	get ....
or put	*or* .... your clothes off

4.6 What are you wearing today? Use a dictionary to help you.

I'm wearing a white T-shirt and a blue jumper. I've got a pair of black trousers on. I'm wearing blue socks and white trainers. I've also got a watch and a pair of glasses on.

5 Describing people

A

Height /haɪt/ and weight /weɪt/

Bettina Schwenke is a very **tall** woman.

Tom Jakes is quite **short**.

If you aren't tall or short, you are of **medium height**.

Agata Sanchez is really **slim**.
I was very **thin** when I was in hospital.
[slim is more polite than thin]

Bettina Schwenke   Tom Jakes

Agata Sanchez

The doctor said I am **overweight**. [weigh too much]

An **overweight** man holding a **fat** cat opened the door.

B

Face and head

Suri has **dark skin** and **dark hair**. She has **brown** eyes.

Polly has **blonde** (or **fair**) **hair** and **fair skin**. She has **blue** eyes.

Beat has **a beard** and **long hair**. He has **green** eyes.

Luca has a **moustache** /mʊˈstɑːʃ/ and **short hair**.

You can also use **has got**, for example, Suri **has got** **dark hair** and **dark skin**.

Polly

Suri

Beat   Luca

> ### Error warning
> People are tall [NOT People are ~~high~~].
> People have blonde or dark hair [NOT ~~hairs~~].

My mother is a very **beautiful** woman. [very pretty]

My dad's a very **good-looking** man.

My sister is **pretty**. (usually girls / women only)

Bob's an **ugly** man. [ugly = the opposite of **beautiful** or **good-looking**]

I'm not ugly or beautiful, I'm just **average-looking**!

C

Age

My grandmother is 97. She's very **old**. My sister is 14. She's **young**, but would like to be **older**. My father is 56. He's **middle-aged**, but would like to be **younger**!

This hospital is for **elderly** people. (more polite than **old**)

D

Expressions

A: **How tall** is Bettina / Tom? B: She's 1.85 metres tall. / He's 1.48 metres tall.

A: **How heavy are you?** / **How much do you weigh?** B: I weigh 62 kilos / 74 kilos, etc.

A: **How old is he?** B: He's 84.

A: **What does** Gemma / your sister **look like?**
B: She's tall and dark. She's very pretty.

> ### Tip
> Some of the words on this page are a little negative, so be careful how you use them. It's better not to say to someone: 'You are fat / thin / ugly / old.'

Exercises

5.1 Complete the sentences.

1 He's only 1 metre 52. He's quite ..short............ .
2 Very .... people are often good at basketball.
3 Models are usually ....
4 Does she have dark skin? No, it's ....
5 She's only seven. She's very ....
6 If I eat too much I'll be ....
7 My grandmother is in this hospital. It's a hospital for .... people. (don't use 'old')

5.2 Complete the questions using the words in brackets ( ).

1 .How tall is your brother?.............. (your brother)
He's about 1 metre 75.
2 Is .... ? (Elena's hair)
No, she's got dark hair.
3 Is .... ? (Mike's hair)
Yes, it is quite long.
4 Are .... ? (your parents)
Not really, they're middle-aged.
5 Is .... ? (his sister)
Yes, she's very pretty.
6 Why .... ? (Sara, so thin)
She's very ill.

5.3 Write sentences about the people in these pictures.

Suzanna   Jeff   Caroline   Stefan

1 Suzanna's .got long blonde hair and fair skin.............
2 Jeff has ....
3 Caroline's got ....
4 Stefan's hair is .... and he ....

5.4 Write questions.

1 your brother, height   .How tall is your brother?............................
2 your teacher, looks   ....
3 you, weight   ....
4 your mother, age   ....
5 your sister, height   ....
6 your parents, looks   ....

5.5 Now write answers to the questions in 5.4.

1 He's not very tall. He's 1 metre 52.

Follow-up

Write down the names of three people you know. Then write about their:
• height (tall, short, medium height)   • eyes (colour)
• hair (colour, long, short, beard)   • looks (ordinary, good-looking, ugly, etc.)

6 Health and illness

A How are you today?

I'm **very well**, thanks.

I'm **fine**, thanks.

I **don't feel very well**. I must go home and rest. (I'll probably be OK tomorrow.)

I **feel ill**. Can you get a **doctor**, please? (Perhaps it's a serious problem.)

That fish was bad. I think I'm going to be **sick**! (I want to vomit.)

B Everyday problems

Have you got **an aspirin**? I've **got a headache**. /'hedeɪk/

I've **got toothache**. /'tu:θ eɪk/ I need to go to the **dentist**.

I'm going to bed with a hot drink. I've **got a cold**.

C Problems people have for many years / all their lives

I get **hay fever** every summer, from flowers and grass. I **sneeze** all day. /sni:z/

My little brother has **asthma**; sometimes he can't breathe. /'æsmə/

D Illnesses in hot / tropical countries

mosquito

In some countries, mosquitoes can give people **malaria**. /məˈleəriə/

The drinking water was bad, and many children had **cholera**. /'kɒlərə/

E Serious illnesses

Every year **cancer** kills many people who smoke. /'kænsə/

Error warning

My father **had a heart attack** [NOT ~~got~~ a heart attack].

F Expressions

A: Do you **have a healthy diet**?
B: Yes, I eat lots of fruit and vegetables.

A: Do you **exercise**?
B: Yes, I like swimming, jogging and cycling. They're really **good for you**.

A: I **feel stressed**!
B: Do you? You need to **relax** more and don't panic about work!

Exercises

6.1 **Complete the dialogues.**

1 A: How are you today?
   B: Very well, thanks. ....
   A: Good!

2 A: Are you OK?
   B: No, ...
   A: Would you like to use the bathroom?
   B: Yes, thank you.

3 A: I ....
   B: I'll get a doctor.
   A: Oh, thank you.

4 A: ....
   B: Here's the dentist's phone number.
   A: Thanks.

5 A: Your nose is red. Have you got ....
   B: Yes.
   A: Have a hot drink and go to bed early.

6.2 **Match the illnesses in the table with a possible treatment.**

go to the dentist	~~take an aspirin~~	go to hospital	go to bed with a hot drink

illness	treatment
a headache	take an aspirin
toothache	
a heart attack	
a cold	

6.3 **What illnesses are connected with …**

1 a mosquito bite? malaria
2 bad drinking water?
3 pollution, traffic fumes, etc.?
4 grass, flowers, etc.?
5 smoking, sunshine, etc.?

6.4 **Answer these questions. Use a dictionary to help you.**

1 Do you have a healthy diet?
2 What exercise do you do?
3 Do you often feel stressed?
4 Have you ever been in hospital?

7 Feelings

A Love, like and hate

++	+	–	– –
love	like	don't like	hate

I **love** my family and my best friend.

I **like** my job.

I **don't like** horror films.

I **hate** spiders.

B Happy, sad and tired

| happy | sad | angry | upset | cold | hot |

| thirsty | hungry | well | ill | tired | surprised |

Error warning

I am very **happy about** your news [NOT I am very ~~happy for~~ your news]. BUT You did very well in your exam – I'm very **happy for you.**

C Prefer, hope and want

I **prefer** coffee **to** tea. (= I **like** coffee **more than** I like tea.)

I **hope to do** well in my exam.

I **hope (that)** my friend does well in his exam.

I **want** a new car. [I would like]

I **want to buy** a new car.

Note: I **want my father to buy** a new car.

Error warning

I want you to help me [NOT I want ~~that you help~~ me].

D Expressions

A: **Do you like** football?
B: Yes, **I really like** football / it. /
   No, **I don't like** football / it very much.

Error warning

[NOT I ~~very like football / it.~~ *or* I ~~like very much football / it.~~]

A: How's your grandfather?
B: He's **very well,** thanks.
A: And **how about** your grandmother?
B: She's **a bit / a little tired.**

Exercises

7.1 Do you love, like, not like or hate these things? Write sentences.

1 chocolate   I love chocolate.
2 cowboy films
3 flying
4 tea

5 football
6 cats
7 cars
8 jazz music

7.2 Which do you prefer? Write answers.

1 tea or coffee?   I prefer coffee to tea.
2 dogs or cats?
3 sunbathing or sightseeing?

4 cars or bikes?
5 strawberry or chocolate ice cream?
6 watching sport or doing sport?

7.3 Answer these questions using *want* or *hope*.

1 You're thirsty. What do you want?   I want a cup of tea.
2 The lesson feels very long. What do you hope?
3 You're hungry. What do you want?
4 Your friend feels ill. What do you hope?
5 You're tired. What do you want to do?
6 You're upset. What do you want to do?
7 It's very cold weather. What do you hope?
8 Your friend feels sad. What do you want?

7.4 Look at the pictures. How do the people feel? Use words from B opposite.

1  Jessica is hungry.

2 Fred ....

3  William ....

4  Sunita ....

5  Fiona ....

6 The children ....

7.5 Correct the mistakes.

1 I very like basketball.   I like basketball very much.
2 I am happy for my sister's good news.
3 The teacher wants that we learn these new words.
4 I like really spiders.
5 My brother has a good new job. I'm very happy about him.
6 My parents want that I go to university.
7 I feel very well. How for you?
8 Priya is bit tired this morning.

Follow-up

When did you last feel ...

1 angry?   2 surprised?   3 upset?   4 hungry?

I felt angry this morning when I read the newspaper.

Conversations 1: Greetings and wishes

Every day

good morning   good afternoon   good evening

Hello

Hi

How are you?

Fine, thanks. And you?

Not too bad, thanks.

Error warning

When it's someone's birthday we say Happy Birthday [NOT ~~Congratulations~~].

When we leave someone we usually say **Goodbye** and also perhaps **See you soon!** See you soon is quite informal.

When someone goes to bed, we usually say **Goodnight**. We sometimes also say **Sleep well**.

Don't say **Goodnight** when you arrive somewhere, only when you leave.

If you ask for something you usually say **Please**.

If someone does something nice for you, you say **Thank you**.

Cheers!   Excuse me!   Sorry!   Bless you!

B ## Special days

When:	you say:
it's someone's birthday	**Happy Birthday!**
it's Christmas	**Happy / Merry Christmas!** /ˈkrɪsməs/
it's New Year's Day	**Happy New Year!**
someone is doing something difficult, e.g. taking an exam or having an interview for a job	**Good luck!**
someone has done something special, e.g. done well in an exam or had a baby	**Congratulations! / Well done!**

Exercises

8.1 Choose one of the phrases from the opposite page to fit the dialogues.

1 A: (*sneezes*) Atishoo!
   B: Bless you! ....

2 A: I'm taking my driving test today.
   B: ....

3 A: I passed my driving test!
   B: ....

4 A: Goodbye.
   B: ....

5 A: It's my birthday today.
   B: ....

6 A: How are you?
   B: ....

7 A: Hello!
   B: ....

8 A: Here's your tea.
   B: ....

8.2 What is the person saying in the pictures?

8.3 What do you say? Choose a phrase from the opposite page.

1 You want to go through a doorway. There are some people blocking it.   Excuse me!
2 A friend buys you a drink.
3 A child says 'Goodnight' to you.
4 You answer the phone at work. It is 10.30 am.
5 You answer the phone at work. It is 3 pm.
6 It is 2 am on January 1st. You meet a friend in the street.
7 You are on a very crowded bus and you stand on someone's foot.
8 It is 24th December. You meet a friend on the bus.

8.4 You meet Ann, an English friend. Reply to her.

ANN: Good evening.
YOU: Hello. ....
ANN: How are you?
YOU: ....
ANN: It's my birthday today.
YOU: ....
ANN: Would you like a drink?
YOU: ....
ANN: Here you are. Cheers!
YOU: ....

8.5 Write a conversation using as many phrases as possible from the opposite page.

9 Conversations 2: Useful words and expressions

A Words

word	example	meaning
actually	People say bad things about her, but she's **actually** very nice.	in reality
really	The book is **really** good.	very
else	Do you want to buy anything **else**? Or go somewhere **else**?	in addition or different
around	I'll meet you at **around** 6 o'clock.	about or approximately
anyway	I'll drive you home. I'm going that way **anyway**.[1] **Anyway**, as I said, I woke up very late today.[2]	[1] to give a reason for doing something [2] to return to an earlier subject

> **Error warning**
> Actually is a false friend in some languages – in English it means 'in reality' NOT 'now'.

B Expressions

A: **Why don't** we go to the cinema this evening? (used to make a suggestion)
B: Good idea. **Let's** go and see a film and then have a meal. (used to make a suggestion)
A: OK! Which film do you want to see?
B: **I don't mind.** [It's all the same to me.] **It's up to you.** [You can decide.]
A: **How about / What about** the new Angelina Jolie film? (used to make a suggestion)
B: Great!

> **Error warning**
> Why don't we go ... [NOT ~~Why don't we going~~] or Let's go ... [NOT ~~Let's going~~].
> How about going ... [NOT ~~How about go~~] or What about going ... [NOT ~~What about go~~].

A: I was late for work today.
B: **Oh dear!** Was your boss angry? (used when you are surprised or disappointed)

A: I forgot to bring your book!
B: Oh, **it doesn't matter.** I don't need it. [it's not important]

A: I'm sorry, but I can't come to your party.
B: **What a pity!** (used when you are disappointed)

A: I passed my exam.
B: **Well done!**

A: **Hurry up!** The taxi's here. [be quick]

A: **Look out! / Be careful!** – there's a car coming.

A: We need to buy Marta's birthday present.
B: **Absolutely!** What about getting her a CD? (used when you agree strongly)
A: **I agree.** Let's go shopping this afternoon.

> **Error warning**
> I agree or I don't agree [NOT ~~I am agree or I'm not agree~~].

Exercises

9.1 Choose a word from A opposite to complete the sentences.

1 It's boring here. Let's go somewhere _else._
2 There were _____ 20 people at the lecture.
3 It's a _____ lovely photo!
4 Have you had enough to eat? Would you like anything _____ ?
5 He said he was a doctor but he's _____ still a medical student.
6 The journey takes _____ two hours.

9.2 Choose the correct answer.

1 I don't like skiing and *about / (anyway) / else* I'm not free that weekend.
2 I don't *mind / matter / agree* what we do. It's all the same to me.
3 *It's up to you / Let's / I agree* invite Rachel to dinner tonight.
4 *Be careful / What a pity / Oh dear* in London. There's lots of traffic there.
5 I don't have time to go to the cinema and *really / absolutely / anyway* I've seen that film already.

9.3 Choose an expression from the box to fit these situations.

Well done!   Oh dear!   What a pity!
Hurry up!   It's up to you.   Look out!

1 Oh dear!
2
3 I didn't get that job.
4 Do you want to go to the party or not?
5
6

9.4 Correct the eight mistakes in the dialogue.

VERA: We need to celebrate. I got a new job!
LUKE: Well ~~made~~! *done*
        How about go out for a meal this evening?
VERA: Great! Let go to that Italian restaurant. Or do you prefer the Chinese one?
LUKE: I don't mind it. I like the Italian one but it's very expensive.
VERA: Oh, it isn't matter.
LUKE: OK. Why don't we going to the Italian restaurant and then we could go to the cinema afterwards? Your new job needs a special celebration.
VERA: I'm agree. And I'd love to see that film with George Clooney. Would you?
LUKE: Absolute!

10 Food and drink

A Everyday food

Would you like some **bread**?

I love sushi because I love **rice**.

Pasta is good for you, but don't eat too much!

I always put **salt** on my **chips,** but not **pepper**.

My sister never eats **meat** or **fish**. She's **vegetarian**.

Do you take **sugar** in **tea** or **coffee**?

> ### Error warning
> Can I have **some bread**? [NOT Can I have ~~a~~ bread?]

B Fast food

I eat **hamburgers, hot dogs** and **pizzas** when I don't have much time.

Fish and chips is popular in Britain, Australia and New Zealand.

C Fruit /fruːt/ and vegetables /ˈvedʒtəbəlz/

Vegetables are good for you. **Fruit** is also good for you. (singular, uncountable)

Vegetables

| carrots | beans | potatoes | tomatoes | peas | onions /ˈʌjənz/ | garlic | mushrooms |

Fruit

orange /ˈɒrɪndʒ/

apple

banana

pear /peə/

grapes

strawberries /ˈstrɔːbrɪz/

pineapple /ˈpaɪnæpl/

> ### Error warning
> I love **fruit** [NOT I love ~~fruits~~].

D Drinks

| tea | coffee | milk | fruit juice | beer | wine | mineral water |

> ### Tip
> Go to a supermarket. How many different kinds of food or drink have English names on them? Try to learn some of them.

Exercises

10.1 Complete the sentences. Use words from the opposite page.

1 Rice............................... is popular in Japan.
2 .... and .... are very popular in Italy.
3 Chips are made from ....
4 Many British people eat ....
5 Hamburgers are made from ....
6 A .... is a sausage inside a piece of bread.

10.2 Put these words into two lists: fruit and vegetables.

~~beans~~ pineapple grapes onions apple carrot garlic pear mushrooms

fruit	vegetables
	beans

10.3 Write the names of these fruit and vegetables.

1 banana............................... 3 .... 5 ....

2 .... 4 .... 6 ....

10.4 Here are the names of some drinks with the letters mixed up. What are they?

1 eta   tea...............................   4 fecofe   ....
2 rebe   ....   5 rituf eciju   ....
3 klim   ....   6 nilemar retaw   ....

10.5 Choose a, b or c.

1 Vegetarians do not eat   a) vegetables   b) meat   c) fast food.
2 Garlic is a kind of   a) fruit   b) fast food   c) vegetable.
3 You put   a) salt   b) beer   c) sugar in coffee.
4 Which is correct   a) pinapple   b) pineapple   c) pieapple?
5 The first sound in onion is the same as the sound in   a) fun   b) orange   c) man.
6 A pear is   a) a drink   b) a vegetable   c) a fruit.

10.6 What are your four favourite foods? And your three favourite drinks? Are they good for you? Use a dictionary to help you.

11 In the kitchen

A What's in the kitchen?

B Things we use in the kitchen

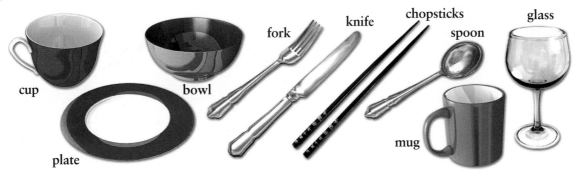

C Things we use for eating and drinking

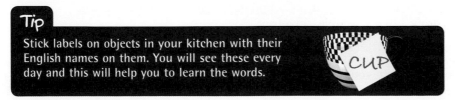

D Expressions

A: **Where can I find** a mug / a cloth / some kitchen paper? B: They are in the cupboard.

A: **Can I help with the** washing-up / cooking? B: Yes, please! You can **dry** the plates. / You can **cook** some rice.

A: **Where does** this cup / plate / frying pan **go**? B: Put it in this cupboard, please.

> **Tip**
>
> Stick labels on objects in your kitchen with their English names on them. You will see these every day and this will help you to learn the words.
>
> CUP

Exercises

11.1 Tick (✓) yes or no. Write sentences for the wrong answers.

		yes	no
1	I use a frying pan to drink out of.		✓
2	You use washing-up liquid to clean plates.		
3	The fridge is cold inside.		
4	The fridge is colder than the freezer.		
5	I turn on the tap to get water.		
6	A tea towel is for making tea.		

11.2 Make questions for these answers. Use words from the opposite page.

1 _Where's the coffee?_ .... It's in the cupboard.
2 .... It's on the cooker.
3 .... Please put them on the worktop.
4 .... Thanks. You can wash these plates and I'll dry them.
5 .... In the fridge on the bottom shelf.

11.3 What do you need?

1 To make coffee I need _a coffee maker, a cup, a spoon._.......
2 To make tea I need ....
3 To fry something I need ....
4 To eat my food I need ....
5 To drink some water I need ....
6 To cook dinner in two minutes I need ....
7 To wash plates, knives and forks I need ....
8 To wash my clothes I need ....

11.4 Look at the picture. Answer the questions.

1 What's on the cooker?   _a saucepan_.....................................
2 What's on the shelf? ....
3 What's in the cupboard under the shelf? ....
4 Where's the microwave? ....
5 What's next to the sink? ....
6 What's under the sink? ....

(See **Unit 52: Places.**)

12 In the bedroom and bathroom

A Bedroom

bedside lamp

hairbrush

comb

dressing table

bed

mirror

chest of drawers

alarm clock

bedside table

wardrobe

pyjamas

B Bathroom

toothpaste

soap

toothbrush

shelf

shower

basin

towel

razor

shampoo

shower gel

toilet

C Joanna's routine

Joanna **goes to bed** at 11 o'clock. She **goes upstairs** to her bedroom.

She **gets undressed** and gets into bed.

She reads for a bit.

She **turns off** the light and **falls asleep**.

She **wakes up** when her alarm clock rings.

She **gets up**.

She **has a shower**, cleans her teeth and gets dressed.

She **goes downstairs** to the kitchen for breakfast.

(See **Unit 45: Everyday things.**)

English Vocabulary in Use Elementary

Exercises

12.1 Look at the picture. Write the words next to the numbers.

2 ....
4 ....
5 ....
6 ....
7 ....
9 ....
1 pyjamas ....
3 ....
8 ....
10 ....

12.2 Write down five more things that you need to take with you if you go to stay with a friend for one night.

toothbrush ....
....
....

12.3 Look at the pictures. Describe what the people are doing.

1 Anne is cleaning her teeth.
3 Mrs Park ....
5 Jaime ....

2 Selim and Umit ....
4 Mr Park ....
6 Lee ....

12.4 What is in your bathroom? Write the things down. Use a dictionary to help you.

12.5 Are these sentences true about your bedroom? If not, change them to make them true.

1 ~~My bedroom is upstairs.~~   My bedroom is not upstairs. I live in a flat.
2 My bedroom has one large window.
3 In my bedroom there is a big bed.
4 There are two wardrobes, one on the left and one on the right of the room.
5 I have a small bedside table.
6 I've got a lamp and an alarm clock on my bedside table.
7 There is a chest of drawers under the window.
8 I haven't got a dressing table.

12.6 Complete this paragraph about your night-time and morning routine.

I usually ¹ go .... to bed at ² .... I get ³ .... and ⁴ .... into bed. I usually read ⁵ .... a bit. I turn ⁶ .... the light and ⁷ .... asleep. I ⁸ .... up when my alarm clock rings. I get ⁹ .... I have a ¹⁰ .... , ¹¹ .... my teeth and ¹² .... dressed. I go to the kitchen for breakfast.

13 In the living room

A Things in the living room

bookshelf (bookshelves) · books · light · light switch · TV · picture · lamp · window · curtains · hi-fi · sofa · socket · table · chair · rug · phone · remote control · carpet · armchair · coffee table

B Useful verbs

Every evening I **watch television**.

Sometimes I **listen to the radio** or **listen to music**.

Sometimes I **read a book**.

Sometimes I **just relax**. [rest and do nothing]

C Expressions

It's getting dark. Can you **close the curtains**, please?

OK. And I'll **switch the light** on.

Thanks. Now can you **turn the radio off**? And **pass me the remote control**. I want to **turn on the TV**. There's a good programme on.

> **Error warning**
>
> The furniture in my room is white [NOT The furniture in my room are white].

Exercises

13.1 **Write the names of …**

1 somewhere you can put books. *a bookshelf*
2 somewhere two or three people can sit.
3 somewhere you can put down your cup.
4 something you can look at on the wall.
5 something for switching the light on or off.
6 something for listening to music.
7 something under your feet.
8 something for changing channels on the TV.

13.2 **Match the words on the left with the words on the right.**

1 switch on the   TV
2 relax in an   lamp
3 close the   remote control
4 pass the   radio
5 listen to the   armchair
6 watch   curtains

13.3 **Correct the mistakes in the sentences.**

1 This evening let's just relax us at home.   *This evening let's just relax at home.*
2 I don't often listen the radio.
3 We need some more bookshelfs in this room.
4 I watched at television all evening yesterday.
5 It's dark now. Please make the curtains.
6 Jim has some very nice furnitures in his house.

13.4 **Find 11 more words from this unit in the wordsearch.**

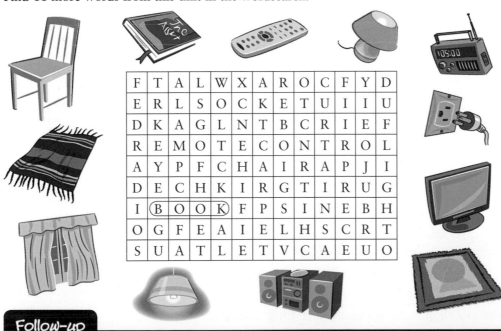

F	T	A	L	W	X	A	R	O	C	F	Y	D
E	R	L	S	O	C	K	E	T	U	I	I	U
D	K	A	G	L	N	T	B	C	R	I	E	F
R	E	M	O	T	E	C	O	N	T	R	O	L
A	Y	P	F	C	H	A	I	R	A	P	J	I
D	E	C	H	K	I	R	G	T	I	R	U	G
I	B	O	O	K	F	P	S	I	N	E	B	H
O	G	F	E	A	I	E	L	H	S	C	R	T
S	U	A	T	L	E	T	V	C	A	E	U	O

Follow-up

Write about your living room at home. You can draw a plan of it first. What furniture is there in the room? What colour are the walls? Are there any pictures on them? What do you do when you are in your living room?

14 Jobs

A What's his/her job?

doctor

teacher

nurse

mechanic

secretary

shop assistant

hairdresser

engineer

farmer

B Jobs in the town

police officer

traffic warden

librarian

bank clerk /klɑːk/

C Expressions

SAM: What's your **job**?

BEN: I'm a **waiter**. I work in a **restaurant**. What do you **do**?

SAM: I'm a **taxi driver**.

BEN: Is it an interesting **job**?

SAM: Yes, I like it. Where do you **work**?

SOPHIE: I work in an **office**. Sometimes it's boring.

My dad works in a **factory** which makes car parts.

I worked in a **shop** at the weekends when I was a student.

I want to work in a **beauty salon** as a **hairdresser**.

I'd like to work in a children's **hospital**.

I'm a writer. I work **at / from** home.

Exercises

14.1 **Where do they work?**

1 A teacher *works in a school / college / university.*
2 A doctor ....
3 A waiter ....
4 A secretary ....
5 A shop assistant ....
6 A hairdresser ....

14.2 **Match the pictures with the jobs in the box.**

| nurse | ~~farmer~~ | secretary | taxi driver | engineer | mechanic |

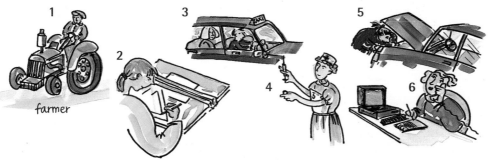

farmer

14.3 **Complete the crossword.**

Across
1 works on a bus
2 works in a school
3 writes books

Down
1 works in a hospital
2 works in a restaurant
3 works with the doctor

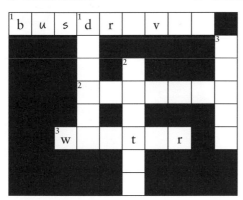

14.4 **Complete the sentences.**

1 He works in a *factory* which makes electrical goods.
2 She's an .... She builds roads and bridges.
3 The traffic .... is checking all the parked cars.
4 The .... told me to return the book at the end of the month.
5 The bank .... changed some money for me.
6 A police .... told me the way to the station.

14.5 **Answer the questions for yourself.**

1 What do you do?
2 Where do you work?
3 Is it an interesting job?

15 At school and university

A Subjects

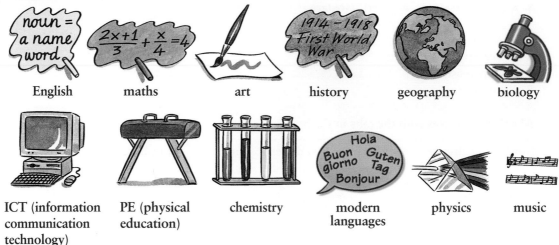

English   maths   art   history   geography   biology

ICT (information communication technology)   PE (physical education)   chemistry   modern languages   physics   music

B Useful things

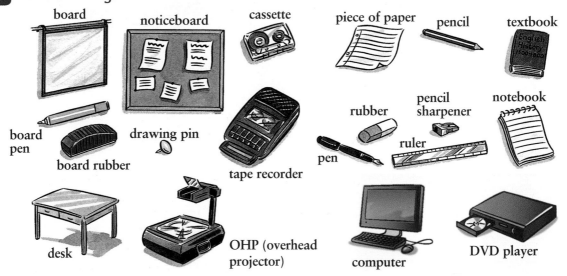

board   noticeboard   cassette   piece of paper   pencil   textbook

board pen   drawing pin   rubber   pencil sharpener   notebook

board rubber   tape recorder   pen   ruler

desk   OHP (overhead projector)   computer   DVD player

C Expressions

A maths **teacher teaches maths**. Her **students study maths**.

Children **go to school** and students **go to university**.

At school children **learn to read and write**.

Students can **do an (English) course** in many schools and universities. At the end of a course, you often **take / do an exam**. You hope to **pass your exams**. You don't want to **fail your exams**.

If you pass your final exams at university, you **get a degree**.

Error warning

After school, students **do homework** [NOT ~~make homework~~ or ~~do homeworks~~]. (See Units 38 and 39 for more expressions with *do* and *make*.)

Exercises

15.1 Match the subject on the left with what you study on the right.

1	maths	a	animals and plants
2	physics	b	sport
3	history	c	$25y + 32x = 51z$
4	geography	d	$e = mc2$
5	PE	e	H_2O
6	English	f	the countries of the world
7	chemistry	g	the 15th century
8	biology	h	computers
9	ICT	i	spelling

15.2 Look at the picture for 30 seconds. Then cover it. How many of the ten objects can you remember? Write them down in English.

15.3 Which of the things in B on the opposite page are in the room where you study English? Write them here.

In the room where I study English I can see ....
....
....

15.4 Choose a verb from C opposite to fill the gaps below. Put the verb in the correct form.

John does well at school. He finds it easy to [1] ...learn........... and he always [2] .... his homework. He usually [3] .... all his exams. He will [4] .... his final school exams soon. If he [5] .... , he will [6] .... to university next year. If he [7] .... , he will be very sad. John really wants to [8] .... geography at university. He would also like to [9] .... a special geology course. His sister is already at university. Next year she will [10] .... her degree and then she will try to find a job.

15.5 Which are/were your three favourite subjects? Which subjects (if any) do / did you not like?

....
....

> **Tip**
>
> Draw two columns on a piece of paper. In one column write five words from the opposite page which you want to learn. In the second column put a drawing (or a translation or a definition). Cover the first column and look at the second column. Can you remember the English words?

16 Communications

A Letters

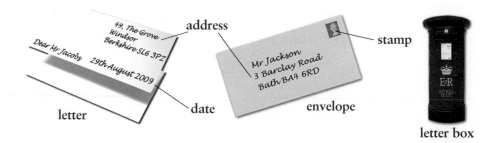

49, The Grove
Windsor
Berkshire SL6 3PZ

address

Dear Mr Jacobs   29th August 2009

stamp

Mr Jackson
3 Barclay Road
Bath BA4 6RD

letter   date   envelope

letter box

Don't forget to put a **stamp** on the **envelope**.

Don't forget to **post** the letters.

B Email and Internet

memory stick

computer   screen   keyboard   mouse   laptop

CD-ROM

Anne gets a lot of **emails** from New York.

You have to be careful what information you give people **online**.

What's your **email address**? Moll@cup.com (= Moll **at** C-U-P **dot** C-O-M)

C Telephones and mobile devices

mobile device   mobile   telephone   phone box

Juan **makes** a lot of **phone calls**. He phones his girlfriend every day.

I always take my PDA with me. I never turn it off.

What's your **phone number**? What's your **mobile** number?

066530718 (= oh six six five three oh seven one eight / oh double six five ...)

He's not answering his phone. I'll leave a **voicemail** and I'll **text** him / **send** him **a text** (**message**).

D Expressions

SUE: Hello.
NICK: Hello. **It's** Nick **here**. Can I **speak to** Ahmed, please?
SUE: I'm sorry, he's not here at the moment.
        Can I **take a message**?
NICK: Thanks. Could you just **tell him I called**. I'll **call back** later.
SUE: OK. I'll tell him. Goodbye.
NICK: Bye.

> **Tip**
> Use a search engine to find an example of a letter and an email in English. Write down any useful words or phrases in them.

Exercises

16.1 Have you got any of the things on the opposite page? Make a list.

mobile

16.2 What are the names of these things?

1 keyboard	4	7	10 ....
2	5	8	11 ....
3	6	9	12 ....

16.3 Complete this phone conversation.

SALLY: Hello.
MEENA: Hello. [1] It's .... Meena here. Can I [2] .... to Amal, please?
SALLY: I'm [3] ...., he's at work [4] .... the moment. Can I [5] ....
a message?
MEENA: It's all right. I'll [6] .... back later.
SALLY: OK, then. Bye.
MEENA: Bye.

16.4 Write down:

1 two telephone numbers that are important to you.

....

2 two email addresses that are important to you.

....

Now read them aloud.

16.5 Answer these questions.

1 Do you prefer to text or phone your friends?
2 Do you send more emails or more text messages?
3 How often do you go online?
4 Do you prefer to use a laptop or a mobile device?
5 Do you often write letters?

17 Holidays

A Holiday (noun)

We **had a** lovely **holiday** in Egypt in 2008.

I'm not working next week. **I'm on holiday**.

Are you **going on holiday** this summer?

B Types of holidays

We're going on **a package holiday** to Hong Kong. (**flights** and hotel are included)

We're going to have a **winter holiday** this year.

I want to go **camping** this year. (sleep in a tent)

I'm going on a **walking holiday** in the Alps.

A **coach tour** is an easy way to go on holiday. (travelling in a comfortable bus)

C Transport

by plane

by car

by ferry

by coach

by train

D Don't forget to take ...

your **passport** (if you are going to another country)

a **visa** (a stamp that you need in your passport to go to some countries)

your **tickets**

some **traveller's cheques** and **currency** (money of the country you are going to)

a **camera**

a **phrasebook**

your **luggage** /ˈlʌgɪdʒ/ (e.g. a **suitcase** or a **rucksack**)

passport

ticket

currency

camera

phrasebook

suitcase

rucksack

E Expressions

A: Are you **flying** to France from England?
B: No, we're going **by ferry**.

A: What are you going to do in Madrid?
B: We want to **try the local food** and **enjoy the nightlife** (clubs, etc.).
A: **Have a great time!** And **send me a postcard!**

(See **Unit 30: Travelling** and **Unit 47: Moving** for more words about travel.)

Exercises

17.1 **Complete the sentences.**

1 A: Are you working on Monday?   B: No, I'm on................. holiday.
2 A: Are you .... on holiday this year?   B: Yes, I'm going camping.
3 A: Did you have a good .... in Greece?   B: Yes, it was wonderful.
4 A: Are you flying to Italy?   B: No, I'm going .... train.
5 A: I'm going to New York next week.   B: Great! Please .... me a postcard.

17.2 **What type of holiday is each person talking about?**

1 It was fun but the tent was very small.   camping................................
2 Everything was included – hotels and flights.   ....
3 We were on the coach for seven days. I was very tired.   ....
4 We walked about 20 kilometres every day.   ....
5 We went to Switzerland in December. There was a lot of snow.   ....

17.3 **Look at the different ways of travelling. Put one tick (✓) for sometimes true, two ticks for often true and three ticks for always true.**

	you can take a lot of luggage	very fast	cheap	you see a lot as you travel	relaxing
ferry					
car	✓✓✓				
plane					

17.4 **Write the names of these things you need for a holiday.**

1 currency................................   3 ....   5 ....

2 ....   4 ....   6 ....

17.5 **What do we call:**

1 something you take photos with? a camera................
2 a special stamp in your passport to enter a country? a v................
3 something you fly in? a p................
4 something that you carry things on your back in? a r................
5 cheques you can use in different countries? t................ c................
6 what people carry their clothes in when they go on holiday? a s................

17.6 **Fill the gaps in this postcard.**

I'm having a great ¹time........ here in Spain. The ²................. is great – the clubs are open all night. The ³................. food is very good – lots of fish and salads. Please send me a ⁴................. from your holiday in Italy.

Love,
Alex

18 Shops and shopping

A Kinds of shops

butcher*

post office

supermarket

bookshop

baker*

chemist*

newsagent*

gift shop

department store

* These words are also for people's jobs. We often add *'s* and say: I'm going to the newsagent's to get a paper. Do you want anything from the butcher's?

B In the department store

A department store is a large shop which sells a lot of different things – clothes, beauty products, toys, etc.

BASEMENT	Electricals Food
GROUND FLOOR	Beauty
FIRST FLOOR	Women's Wear
SECOND FLOOR	Men's Clothes Children's Department
THIRD FLOOR	Furniture
FOURTH FLOOR	Toys Restaurant

C Signs in shops

OPEN

CLOSED

Cash desk
Please pay here

PUSH

PULL

D Expressions

SHOP ASSISTANT:	Can I help you?
CUSTOMER:	Can I **try this shirt on**? (*goes and tries it on*) Have you got a **bigger** / **smaller** size / a **different colour**?
SHOP ASSISTANT:	No, I'm sorry. That's the only one.
CUSTOMER:	OK. I'll take it. How much does it **cost**?
SHOP ASSISTANT:	£17.
CUSTOMER:	Can I **pay** by **cheque**?
SHOP ASSISTANT:	No, **credit card** or **cash** only.
CUSTOMER:	Sorry, I only have a £50 **note**. I don't have any **change**. [coins or smaller notes]
SHOP ASSISTANT:	That's OK. Here's your **receipt**. Would you like a (**carrier**) **bag**?

Exercises

18.1 Match the item with the shop.

| toy shop | butcher | ~~chemist~~ | baker | gift shop | newsagent |

1 aspirin

2 beach ball

3 sausages

4 postcards

5 souvenir T-shirt

6 bread

18.2 Where do you need to go?

1 I want to get a newspaper.   *the newsagent*
2 I'd like to buy food for a week.
3 I need some stamps.
4 We must get Jim a present.
5 I'd like to buy a book.
6 I want to buy some clothes for myself and my children in one shop.

18.3 Look at the department store plan in B opposite. Which floor will you go to buy:

1 an armchair? *third floor*
2 lipstick? ....
3 a cup of tea? ....
4 a packet of tea? ....
5 a skirt? ....

6 some baby clothes? ....
7 a tie? ....
8 a TV? ....
9 a bed? ....
10 a doll? ....

18.4 Write the words for these definitions.

1 a person who sells things in a shop   *shop assistant*
2 money (not a cheque or credit card)
3 a piece of paper that is worth £20
4 'plastic money'
5 coins or small notes

Now write definitions in English for these words/phrases.

6 a butcher's
7 the first floor
8 a newsagent's
9 the basement

18.5 Which sign tells you ...

1 that you can give the money for the things you are buying here?   *Cash desk*
2 that you can't go into the shop?
3 that the door will open towards you?
4 that the door will open away from you?
5 that you can go into the shop?

18.6 Fill the gaps in the dialogue.

CUSTOMER: How much does this jacket [1]............................. ?
SHOP ASSISTANT: £50.
CUSTOMER: I'll take it, please. Can I [2]............................. by credit card?
SHOP ASSISTANT: Certainly. I'll put your receipt in the [3]............................. .

19 In a hotel

A Places and things in the hotel

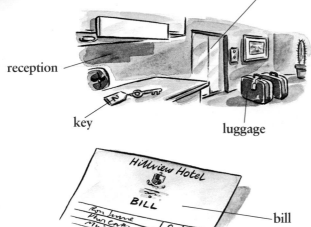

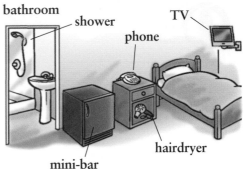

reception

key

luggage

lift

form

bill

bathroom

shower

phone

TV

hairdryer

mini-bar

B Expressions in reception

Do you have a **single room** [for one person] / a **double room** [for two people]?

I have a **reservation**. [I booked a room] My name is …

We'd like a **room with a view** of the sea.

The receptionist may say:

Here is your key.

Your room is **on the first floor. Take the lift.** It's **over there.**

Would you like **some help with your luggage?**

Can you **fill in this form,** please?

Sign (your name) here, please. [write your name]

Please **check your bill.** [make sure it is correct]

When you leave you say:

Can I **check out,** please?

Can I have the **bill,** please?

C Asking questions about hotel services

How much is a single room with a **bathroom?**

Can I order **room service?**

How do I **get an outside line?** (You want to phone someone who is not in the hotel.)

What is **the code for** Poland?

Can I **have breakfast in my room,** please?

Can I **have a wake-up call** at 6.30, please? (You want to wake up at 6.30.)

What time is breakfast / lunch / dinner?

Can I **(ex)change some money,** please?

Exercises

19.1 Look at the pictures and complete the dialogue with words from the opposite page.

CUSTOMER: Can I have a ¹ *double* room for tonight, please?

RECEPTIONIST: Would you like a room with a ² .... ?

CUSTOMER: Yes, please. And with a ³ .... , please.

RECEPTIONIST: All our rooms have a TV, a ⁴ .... and a

 ⁵ .... I can give you room 25. It has a view of the

 ⁶ .... Here is your ⁷ .... The

 ⁸ .... is over there. The room's on the second floor.

19.2 Match what you want on the left with what you need on the right.

You want:
1 to have a drink in your room
2 to go to the top floor
3 to open your door
4 to get up at 6 am
5 to phone your country
6 to watch the news
7 to wash your hair
8 to dry your hair

You need:
a the lift
b an outside line
c a shower
d a mini-bar
e a hairdryer
f a wake-up call
g a TV
h a key

19.3 Choose the right words to complete these sentences.

1 At *reception* / *reservation* you can order *room* / *lift* service.
2 We'd like a *two* / *double* room with a *view* / *see* of the garden, please.
3 The lift is *after* / *over* there. Take it to the second *floor* / *room*.
4 Please *fill* / *write* in this *form* / *bill*.
5 I'd like a *sit-up* / *wake-up* call at 7.30 and I'd like to *make* / *have* breakfast in my room, please.
6 I have a *luggage* / *reservation* for a *single* / *one* room with a bathroom.
7 Can I *cash* / *have* the bill, please? I'll *check* / *change* it now.
8 I'm leaving today. Can I *exchange* / *order* some dollars here before I *pay* / *check* out?

19.4 Write down questions that you can ask in a hotel beginning: Can I ... ? Use these words.

wake-up call   *Can I have a wake-up call, please?*
breakfast in my room   bill   double room   luggage

19.5 Answer the questions.

1 How much does a hotel room cost in the capital of your country?
2 What is the code for Britain if you phone from your country?
3 What time is breakfast usually in a hotel in your country?
4 Is it most important for you to have a hairdryer, a TV or a mini-bar in a hotel room?

20 Eating out

Places where you can eat

café: you can **have a cup of tea / coffee** and a **snack** there (e.g. a sandwich or a cake). They sometimes serve **meals** (e.g. lunch, dinner) too.

restaurant: you go there for a meal; more expensive than a café.

bar / pub: bars and pubs serve **alcohol** and **soft drinks** [non-alcoholic drinks, e.g. fruit juice]; you can usually have a meal or a snack there too.

fast food restaurant: you can get a quick hot meal there, for example burger and chips.

take-away: you buy a snack or a meal there and take it home to eat.

B In a restaurant

Menu

Starters
Soup of the day (v)
Mixed salad (v)

Main courses
Steak with chips or new potatoes
Fish and chips
Vegetable curry (v)
Salmon fillet with green beans
Burger with chips and mushrooms

Desserts
Chocolate ice cream
Apple pie
Fruit salad
(v = vegetarian)

C Expressions

WAITER: Are you **ready to order**?
CUSTOMER: Yes, **I'd like** the steak, please.
WAITER: **Would you like** it with chips or new potatoes?
CUSTOMER: With chips, please.
WAITER: **How would you like** your steak – **rare**, **medium** or **well-done**?
CUSTOMER: Well-done, please.
WAITER: And **what would you like to drink**?
CUSTOMER: **I'll have** a coke, please.
(later)
WAITER: **Is everything all right**?
CUSTOMER: Thank you, it's **delicious**. [very good]
(later)
CUSTOMER: **Could I have the bill**, please?
WAITER: Yes, of course.

Exercises

20.1 Look at A opposite. Where would you go to …

1 buy a meal and take it home to eat?   _a take-away_
2 have a romantic dinner for two?   ....
3 eat a quick lunch?   ....
4 have a cake and a cup of coffee?   ....
5 drink a glass of wine with friends?   ....

20.2 Write down the name of a place of this type in your town.

1 fast food restaurant: ..McDonald's..
2 café: ....
3 take-away: ....
4 restaurant: ....
5 bar: ....

20.3 Choose one of the words in the box which can go with each of the words in each group.

> steak   curry   pie   ~~soup~~   salad

1 You can have tomato / vegetable / chicken .soup................. as a starter.
2 I'd like the beef / chicken / vegetable .... as a main course.
3 I'll have the mixed / tomato / fruit ....
4 Can I have the apple / chicken .... , please.
5 Do you like your .... well-done, medium or rare?

20.4 Correct the six mistakes in this dialogue.

WAITER: Are you ready ~~for~~ order?   _to_
CUSTOMER: Yes. I like vegetable soup and steak, please.
WAITER: What would you like your steak? Rare, medium or done good?
CUSTOMER: Rare, please.
WAITER: What you would like to drink?
CUSTOMER: A orange juice, please.

20.5 Cover the menu opposite. Write the food you can remember. Look at the menu again and check your answers.

20.6 Answer these questions.

1 What would you choose to eat from the menu opposite?
2 What can vegetarians eat from the menu?
3 Do you like eating out?
4 How often do you go to a restaurant?

Follow-up

Sometimes restaurants in other countries have English menus for tourists. Look at one of these. Write down any useful words you find.

21 Sports

A | Ball games

We **play** all these sports.

football

rugby

American football

basketball

badminton

baseball

tennis

volleyball

table tennis

B | Other popular sports

swimming

running

sailing

motor racing

horse racing

judo / karate

snowboarding

skiing

kayaking

We can use **go** with all the sports listed in B, apart from judo and karate. I **go** running every day. I **went** skiing last year. We use **do** with judo and karate. She **does** judo.

(See **Unit 37**: Go / went /gone.)

C | Where we do sports

We play tennis / badminton / volleyball / basketball on a **tennis / badminton / volleyball / basketball court.**

We play football / rugby on **a football / rugby pitch.**

We swim in a **swimming pool.**

Many towns have **a sports centre** – you can do lots of different sports there.

D | Expressions

Do you do any sports? Yes, **I go** swimming / running / sailing / kayaking.

Do you play football / tennis / badminton? I **play** tennis. Which sports do you play?

What's your favourite sport? I **like** motor racing **best.**

Exercises

21.1 Cover the opposite page. What are these sports?

1 rugby

3 ....

5 ....

2 ....

4 ....

6 ....

21.2 Which sports use these things?

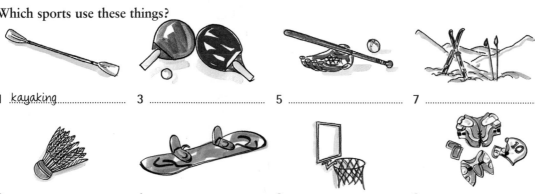

1 kayaking

3 ....

5 ....

7 ....

2 ....

4 ....

6 ....

8 ....

21.3 Ask questions for these answers.

1 Where do people play tennis?
   On a tennis court.

2 Do you ....
   Yes, but only American football.

3 ....
   No, I don't do any at all. I prefer watching TV.

4 Do you ....
   Yes, I go to the swimming pool every Friday.

5 What ....
   I like running best.

6 Where ....
   On a rugby pitch.

21.4 Look at the different sports in this unit.

1 Write the names of the sports you have done.   ....

2 Where did you do them?   ....

3 Which ones do you like?   ....

4 Which do you not like?   ....

5 Which ones would you like to do?   ....

Follow-up

Make a page in your vocabulary book for 'sports'. Look at the sports pages of an English-language newspaper. Write down the names of sports you do not know. Look them up in a dictionary.

22 Cinema

A Types of films

a western

a horror film

an action film

a musical

a cartoon

a thriller

a comedy

a science fiction film

a romantic comedy

B People in films

Zelda Glitzberg is a **film star**.

She lives in Hollywood.

She is **in** the new James Bond film.

Daniel Radcliffe **played** Harry Potter in the Harry Potter films.

I like films by Italian **directors**.

C Expressions

Error warning

Do you **go to the cinema** often? [NOT ~~Do you go to cinema often?~~]

Yes, I go every week.
No, I **watch DVDs** at home.

Error warning

What's **on at** the cinema this week? [NOT ~~What's on the cinema this week?~~]

There's a comedy with Cameron Diaz.

A: Have you **seen** the latest James Bond film?
B: Yes, I saw it **on TV**.

A: Did you like the new *Batman* film?
B: Yes, **I loved it / enjoyed it.** /
   No, it was **boring**.

A: Do you like **westerns**? B: No, I like **science fiction films** best.

The best **action film** I've seen was *Quantum of Solace* with Daniel Craig.

If I see a **horror film,** I can't sleep.

Exercises

22.1 **What types of films are these?**

1 Some cowboys rob a train.   western
2 A flying saucer lands from Mars.
3 A dead person comes back to life.
4 James Bond saves the world.
5 Mickey Mouse goes on a picnic.
6 A man falls in love with his teacher.
7 A dead body is found in the river.
8 There are lots of songs and dancing.

22.2 **Write the name of a film of each type.**

1 science fiction   War of the Worlds
2 romantic comedy   ....
3 thriller   ....
4 western   ....
5 musical   ....
6 cartoon   ....

22.3 **Word puzzle. Can you make words for other types of films with the letters of ROMANTIC?**

```
        T H R I L L E R
          ...... O ...... ...... ...... R
      C ...... M ...... ...... Y
          A ...... T ...... ...... N
  S ...... ...... ...... N C ...... F ...... ...... ...... ...... ...... N
      W ...... ...... T ...... ...... N
      M ...... ...... I C ...... L
          C A ...... ...... O O ......
```

22.4 **Fill the gaps in these sentences.**

1 Do you prefer going to the .... cinema or watching TV?
2 We .... a DVD last night.
3 Who .... James Bond in *You Only Live Twice*?
4 Was Matt Damon .... *The Bourne Ultimatum*?
5 Lots of big .... live in Hollywood.
6 Steven Spielberg is a famous American film ....

22.5 **Answer these questions.**

1 What is your favourite type of film?
2 Who is your favourite film star?
3 Do you prefer going to the cinema or watching DVDs?
4 What was the last film you saw?
5 How can you find out what is on at the cinema where you live or study?

Follow-up

Go to the *Time* magazine website of the 100 best films in the world http://www.time.com/time/2005/100movies/the_complete_list.html. Choose three English-language films you would like to see.

23 Free time at home

A TV, radio, music, film

I **watch TV** every evening.

Did you **watch / see** the film about President Kennedy?

What **programmes** do you like best on TV and radio?

I like **watching** films on TV. (You can also say: I like to watch …)

At the weekend, we usually **watch a DVD**.

I like **listening to** music on the radio. (You can also say: I like to listen …)

I often **listen to CDs** or my **MP3 player** when I'm relaxing.

I need some new **headphones** for my MP3 player.

B Hobbies

A lot of young people **play computer games** every day.

How often do you use **the Internet**?

I **download** music and films from the Internet.

I **chat to my friends online** every evening.

I really like **cooking**.

Do you like **gardening**? /ˈɡɑːdnɪŋ/

We **grow flowers** and **vegetables** in our garden.

C Reading

I read a lot at home.

What do you read?

I read **novels**. [long stories] My sister likes **comics**.

I like **books about** nature and different countries.

I like **magazines about** rock music and sport.

Do you read a **newspaper** every day?

D Expressions

We sometimes **have friends round**.

[we ask them to come to our house / flat]

I often **have friends to dinner**.

My best friend **comes to stay** sometimes.

[sleeps in my house / flat]

I **talk to** my friends **on the phone** every evening.

Sometimes, I just **do nothing**.

Grandpa likes to **have a sleep** after lunch.

> ### Error warning
> We watch TV [NOT ~~see TV~~] and we listen to the radio [NOT ~~hear or listen the radio~~].

Exercises

23.1 What are these people doing?

1 She's _watching TV._ .... 3 He's .... a 5 She's using the ....
....

2 He's .... 4 She's .... 6 He's ....
to ....

23.2 Fill in the missing verbs.

1 Sometimes I _listen_................ to CDs or an MP3 player.
2 I like .... magazines more than newspapers.
3 I .... to my sister on the phone every Sunday.
4 A lot of people like to .... a sleep after lunch.
5 Do you ever .... friends to dinner?
6 The children .... computer games every evening.
7 I want to .... some music from the Internet this evening.
8 Did you .... the programme about Namibia yesterday?
9 My dad .... vegetables in his garden.
10 Shall we .... a DVD tonight?

23.3 Answer these questions.

1 When you have friends round, what do you like to do?
2 Who comes to stay at your house / flat?
3 What do you like to read most?
4 How often do you talk to your friends on the phone?
5 Do you have an MP3 player? How often do you use it?
6 How often do you chat to your friends online?
7 Do you ever download music or films from the Internet?
8 What is your favourite computer game?
9 When do you use headphones?

23.4 Interesting or boring? Number these activities from 5 (= very interesting) to 1 (= very boring).

| gardening | cooking | reading | using the Internet | watching DVDs |
| listening to music | doing nothing | chatting online | | |

24 Music and musical instruments

A Music, musical and musician

Music is an uncountable noun. We do not use it in the plural.

The band played fantastic **music** for more than two hours [NOT fantastic ~~musics~~].

Musical is an adjective.

There is a shop on King Street that sells **musical** instruments [NOT ~~music instruments~~].

A **musician** (noun) is a person.

My brother is a very good **musician**. He plays three instruments.

B Musical instruments

piano   guitar   violin   clarinet

cello   flute   trumpet   drums

C Playing musical instruments

Connie **plays the clarinet**. Her brother **plays the drums**.

Krishnan **is learning the guitar**. His friend, Alba, **has piano lessons**.

Wilma is a very good **flute-player**. She **plays in an orchestra**. Her friend, Nuria, is a good **trumpet-player**.

Ricardo is an excellent **violinist**. His sister is a good **pianist**.

Can you **play a musical instrument**?

D Listening to music

Kim **loves classical music**. (for example, Beethoven, Mozart) [NOT ~~classic music~~]

Marsha **can't stand opera**. [dislikes it very much] She prefers **pop** music.

I like **folk music**, **jazz** and **rock**.

I often **listen to my MP3 player** on the train.

I **downloaded some new songs** yesterday. Do you want to hear them?

> ### Error warning
> A band means a group of musicians. We do not say 'a music band'.
> Nuala had a really good band at her 21st birthday party.
> A concert means an event with music. We do not say a 'music concert'.
> We're going to a concert tonight.

Exercises

24.1 Choose the correct word: *music*, *musical* or *musician*.

1 What are your favourite types of .....music.......... ?
2 My brother thinks he's a good .... , but he's very bad!
3 Can you play a .... instrument?
4 I love different types of .... , for example, jazz, rock and classical.
5 Which .... instrument would you like to learn?
6 Are there any .... in your family?

24.2 Look at the pictures and complete the sentences.

Alex   Donna   Suzanna   Chunshen

Emma   Patricia   William   Bethan

1 Suzanna plays the ....violin............... .
2 .... plays the cello in an ....
3 Chunshen loves playing the ....
4 Donna is having a .... lesson.
5 Alex is a very good ....-player.
6 Bethan plays the .... every evening.
7 William .... the ....
8 Emma is learning the .... She will be a good flute-............................. one day.
9 .... is a violinist.
10 .... wants to be a pianist.

24.3 Choose the correct answer, a, b or c.

1 I love   a) classic   b) classical   c) classist   music. Beethoven is my favourite.
2 My brother   a) can't stand   b) can stand   c) can't stay   folk music but I love it.
3 I have some tickets for a   a) concert music   b) music concert   c) concert   at the Town Hall.
  Would you like one?
4 I always   a) listen in   b) listen to   c) listen   my MP3 player when I'm studying.
5 My sister plays in a   a) music band   b) band music   c) band   with three other girls from
  her school.

24.4 Answer these questions.

1 How often do you download music?
2 Which musical instrument on the opposite page do you like best?
3 Can you play a musical instrument?
4 Which musical instrument would you like to learn?
5 Do you prefer classical music or pop music?

25 Countries and nationalities

A Continents and countries

continent	country	continent	country
North America	Canada	Australasia	Australia
	USA / the US		New Zealand
South America	Argentina	Asia	China
	Brazil		India
	Chile		Japan
	Colombia		Pakistan
	Peru		Thailand
Europe	Germany	Africa	Egypt
	Italy		Morocco
	Poland		South Africa
	Spain		Tunisia
	the UK	Antarctica	

It is not possible to show all the countries of the world on a small page. If your country is not included, check its English name with your teacher or on the Internet.

Error warning

All the nouns and adjectives in this unit always begin with a capital letter, for example Africa [NOT africa].

B Nationalities

notes	adjective
most country adjectives end in *(i)an*	American, Argentinian, Australian, Brazilian, Canadian, Colombian, Egyptian, German, Indian, Italian, Moroccan, Peruvian, South African, Tunisian
many country adjectives end in *ish*	British, English, Finnish, Irish, Polish, Scottish, Spanish
a few country adjectives end in *ese*	Chinese, Japanese, Portuguese
exceptions	Pakistani, Thai

Tip

Remember that words for languages are often the same as the 'people' adjective, e.g. **French, Spanish, Japanese** and **Thai**. One exception is **Arabic**.

Exercises

25.1 **Which countries do these letters make?**

1 H I N A C *China*   4 O C R M O O C
2 Z I R A L B   5 A N J A P
3 P I N S A   6 D A L T H I N A

25.2 **Match these capital cities to their countries and make sentences.**

1 Tokyo *Tokyo is the capital of Japan.*
2 Rome
3 Canberra
4 Bogotá
5 Cairo
6 London
7 Berlin
8 Warsaw
9 Buenos Aires
10 Madrid

| Argentina Australia Colombia |
| Egypt Germany Italy ~~Japan~~ |
| Poland Spain the UK |

25.3 **Which country is different? (Think of the languages they speak there.) Write sentences.**

1 Australia, Canada, England, Iceland   *In England, Canada and Australia they speak English but in Iceland they speak Icelandic.*

2 Brazil, Chile, Mexico, Spain
3 Austria, Germany, Italy, Switzerland
4 China, Egypt, Morocco, Saudi Arabia
5 Canada, France, Scotland, Switzerland

25.4 **What is the adjective for these countries?**

1 Indian *Indian*   6 Spain
2 Thailand   7 Peru
3 Germany   8 China
4 Egypt   9 Australia
5 Argentina   10 Poland

25.5 **Write down:**

1 the name of your country.
2 the names of the countries next to your country.
3 the name of your language.
4 the name for people from your country.

Follow-up

In which continents are these places? Use the Internet to help you.

Mount Everest *Asia*
the Sahara
the Amazon
Wagga Wagga
the Volga
Mount Kilimanjaro
the Mississippi
Mount Fuji
Lake Titicaca

26 Weather

A Types of weather

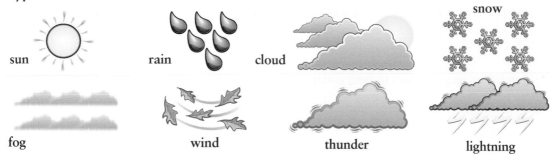

sun rain cloud snow

fog wind thunder lightning

B Adjectives and verbs

noun	adjective
sun	sunny
rain	rainy
wind	windy
cloud	cloudy
snow	snowy
fog	foggy
thunder	thundery
lightning	–

C Other useful weather words

It is very **hot** in Mexico – it is often **45 degrees** there in summer.

It is very **cold** in the Arctic – it is often **minus 50 degrees** there.

It can be very **wet** in London – carry an umbrella when you go sightseeing there.

It is very **dry** in the Sahara – it doesn't often rain there.

A **hurricane** is a very strong wind.

A **storm** is when there is a strong wind and rain together.

A **thunderstorm** is when there is thunder, lightning, rain and sometimes wind together.

D Expressions

It's a sunny day in Tokyo today, but **it's cloudy** in Hong Kong.

It's foggy in Sydney and **it's snowing / it's snowy** in Moscow.

It's raining in Barcelona but **the sun is shining** in Granada.

It's a lovely day.

It's a horrible day, isn't it!

What's the weather like in your country in June?

It's usually warm and sunny.

> **Error warning**
>
> We say It's windy / cloudy / foggy / sunny [NOT It's ~~winding~~ / ~~clouding~~ / ~~fogging~~ / ~~sunning~~].

> **Tip**
>
> Watch the weather forecast in English on TV or online as often as you can.

Exercises

26.1 Match the words and the symbols.

1 snow   2 sun   3 rain   4 fog   5 lightning   6 wind   7 cloud

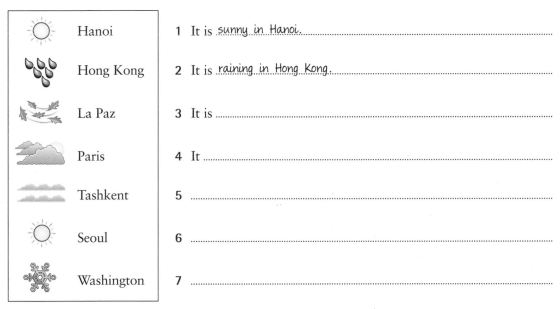

26.2 Look at the chart. Write sentences about the cities in the chart.

Hanoi

Hong Kong

La Paz

Paris

Tashkent

Seoul

Washington

1 It is _sunny in Hanoi._ ....

2 It is _raining in Hong Kong._ ....

3 It is ....

4 It ....

5 ....

6 ....

7 ....

26.3 Complete these sentences with a word from the opposite page.

1 The sun _shone_............... every day last month.
2 When it .... , I take my umbrella.
3 What's the .... like in your country in January?
4 When it .... , we can go skiing.
5 You see .... before you hear thunder.
6 It is 24 .... here today.
7 It is dangerous to be in a small boat at sea in a ....
8 It is very .... in Siberia in winter.

26.4 Are these sentences true about the weather in your country? If not, correct them.

1 It often snows in December. _It sometimes snows in December._
2 It is usually 40 degrees in summer and minus 20 degrees in winter.
3 There are thunderstorms every day in August.
4 It is very wet in spring.
5 We never have hurricanes.
6 Summer is usually hot and dry.

26.5 What do you like to do or not like to do in these types of weather?

1 fog _I don't like to drive._   3 a rainy day   5 a windy day
2 sunny weather   4 snow

27 In the town

A

A Places in the town

Train station / railway station – you can **get a train** here.

Bus station – you can **get a bus** here.

Shops – you can buy things here. (See **Unit 18: Shops and shopping.**)

Shopping centre – area of town with a lot of shops.

Tourist information office – tourists can **get information** here.

Museum – you can see interesting old things here.

Bank – you can **change money** here or get money from **a cash machine**.

Post office – you can **post letters and parcels** here.

Library /ˈlaɪbrəri/ – you can **read books** and **newspapers** here.

Town hall – local government officers work here.

Car park – you can **park your car** here.

Pedestrian area /ˈeəriə/ – you can only walk here, you can't come here by car.

B Notices in towns

EXIT

ENTRANCE

No smoking

PLEASE DO NOT WALK ON THE GRASS

OUT OF ORDER

C Asking for and giving directions

A: **Where is** the bus station?
B: **Go left** here and it's **at the end of the road**.

A: **How do I get to** Market Street?
B: **Take the first right** and then the second left.

A: **Is there** a shopping centre near here?
B: Yes, **turn right** here. The entrance is on Market Street **on the left**.

A: **Can I** park here?
B: No, but **there's a** car park on Park Street.

A: Excuse me, **I'm looking for** the museum.
B: It's on Bridge Road. **Take the number 31 bus** and **get off at the** second **stop**.

A: **Can you tell me the way to** the nearest bank, please? I need a **cash machine**.
B: No problem. Go left here and there's one **on the other side of the road**.

Exercises

27.1 **Answer the questions.**

1 Where can I get a bus to London? *at the bus station*
2 Where can I get information about hotels?
3 Where can I change money?
4 Where can I park my car?
5 Where can I see old and interesting things?
6 Where can I get a train?
7 Where can I go to a lot of different shops?
8 Where can I read today's newspaper? (I don't want to buy it.)

27.2 **Which notice from B opposite will help you?**

1 The cash machine doesn't give you any money. *Out of order*
2 You are in the shopping centre and you want to leave.
3 You want to sit in a place where there are no cigarettes.
4 You want to know if people can go on the grass.
5 You want to go into the museum.

27.3 **Complete these sentences.**

1 Turn right at the *end* of the road.
2 The bus .... is over there .... the left.
3 For the Town Hall .... the number 14 bus.
4 .... is a post office on the other .... of the road.
5 You can find a cash .... at the bank in High Street.
6 We can get a map of the town at the tourist .... office.
7 Can you tell me the .... to the railway .... , please?
8 .... me. I'm looking .... a car park.

27.4 **What words are these?**

1 sumuem *museum*	6	dtaeepsrin raae
2 nowt hlal	7	scah enicmah
3 brilyra	8	tsop ffcoie
4 rac prak	9	phoss
5 ywrlaai nttoisa	10	sub post

27.5 **Look at the map in C opposite. How do you get from the tourist information office to the shopping centre? Write directions.**

27.6 **Does your town have these places? Where are they? Write sentences.**

1 a train station *There's a train station. It's at the end of Station Road.*
2 a bus station   5 a town hall   8 a museum
3 a shopping centre   6 a pedestrian area   9 a post office
4 a library   7 a tourist information office

> **Tip**
> Keep a notebook in your pocket. Many towns in different countries have notices in English to help tourists. Write down any English words and expressions that you see in your town.

28 In the countryside

The **countryside** and the **country** both mean 'not the city'. **Country** can also mean a nation (e.g. France, China).

A Things we can see in the countryside

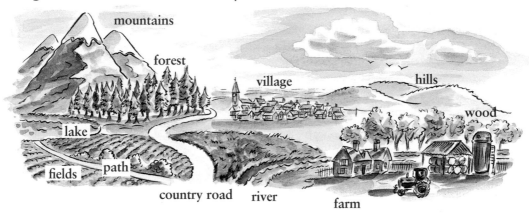

mountains
forest
village
hills
wood
lake
fields
path
country road
river
farm

B Living and working in the countryside

In the countryside, people usually live in a **small town** (e.g. 6,000 people) or **village** /ˈvɪlɪdʒ/ (e.g. 700 people).

A **farmer** lives **on a farm** and works in the fields.

My friend lives in a **cottage**. /ˈkɒtɪdʒ/ [small house in a village or the countryside]

C Nature /ˈneɪtʃə/ and conservation /kɒnsəˈveɪʃn/

Nature means 'everything in the natural world'. (= animals, birds, plants, etc.)

> ### Error warning
>
> I love **nature** [NOT I love ~~the~~ nature]. I like walking **in the countryside** [NOT I like walking in the ~~nature~~]. 'Nature' is not a place.

There is wonderful **wildlife** in the north of the country. [animals, birds, fish and insects]

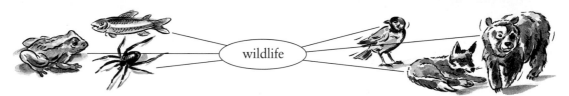

wildlife

Near the village there is **a conservation area**. [place where wildlife and nature are protected]

In the south of the country, there is a **national park**. [very big national conservation area]

D Things to do in the countryside

You can take food and drink and **have a picnic**.

You can **go walking / skiing** in the mountains.

Exercises

28.1 Cover the opposite page. How many names of things in the countryside can you remember?

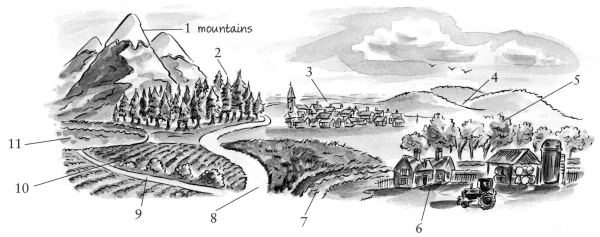

28.2 Fill the gaps in these sentences.

1 My brother is a farmer. He lives on a ..farm............... .
2 It's not a big house; it's just a ....
3 The farm is near a .... which has 800 people.
4 Twenty kilometres from the village there is a small .... It has 9,000 people.

28.3 Match the beginning of the sentences on the left with the ends of the sentences on the right.

1 We went swimming   sitting by the river.
2 We went walking   in the national park.
3 We went skiing   in the lake. The water was warm.
4 We saw some wonderful wildlife   along a five-kilometre path.
5 We had a picnic   down the mountain.

28.4 Put *the* in the sentences if necessary.

1 My parents live in ..the................ countryside.
2 He loves .... nature.
3 She wants to live in .... country.
4 They are interested in .... wildlife.

28.5 Describe the typical countryside where you come from. Write eight sentences about it.
Use these questions to help you.

1 Are there any woods or forests?   There are some big forests.
2 Are there any hills or mountains?
3 Are there any lakes or rivers?
4 Are there many villages or small towns?
5 Are there farms?
6 Are there paths where you can walk?
7 Can you go skiing?
8 Can you see wildlife?

29 Animals

A Farm animals

horse

pig

chicken / hen

sheep

cow

goat

animal	produce	baby
horse	hair, meat	foal
cow	milk, leather, meat (beef)	calf
sheep	wool, meat (lamb)	lamb
pig	meat (pork, bacon, ham)	piglet
chicken / hen	eggs, meat (chicken)	chick
goat	milk, goatskin, meat	kid

B Wild or zoo animals

elephant

monkey

tiger

giraffe

snake

lion

C Pets

These animals are often **pets**.

fish

rabbit

tortoise

cat

parrot

dog

A parrot is a **bird**.

D Expressions

Take your dog **for a walk** every day.

You must **feed your animals** and **give them water** every day.

Do you have any pets?

Exercises

29.1 Complete these sentences.

1 A <u>tortoise</u> goes to sleep in winter.
2 A .... has a very long neck.
3 .... and .... are birds.
4 .... and .... are large cats.
5 You can ride a .... and an ....
6 .... swim and .... fly.
7 .... are farm birds.
8 .... are very good at hopping and jumping.
9 Don't forget to .... the cat and to .... it some water.
10 I .... my dog for a walk every day before school.

29.2 Match the animal with its meat and with its young animal.

animal	meat	young
goat	lamb	calf
sheep	chicken	piglet
cow	pork	lamb
hen	beef	kid
pig	goat	chick

29.3 Look at the animals opposite. Find three animals which:

1 eat meat.   <u>lions,</u> ....
2 give us things that we wear.   ....
3 produce their babies in eggs. ....
4 we can eat.   ....

29.4 Look at the pictures and complete the crossword.

Across

Down

29.5 There are 18 different animals in the pictures on the opposite page. Close the book.
How many of these animals can you remember?

30 Travelling

A Types of transport

train   (aero)plane   car   bus   bicycle / bike   taxi

motorbike / motorcycle   underground   boat   ship   helicopter

B Useful travel words

map   timetable   customs   luggage   passport

Can I have a **single / return** (ticket) to Barcelona, please?
(single = Madrid to Barcelona; return = Madrid to Barcelona and back to Madrid)

I'd like to **book / reserve a seat in advance**. [to make sure you have a seat]

> **Error warning**
> Was the **journey** long? [NOT Was the ~~travel~~ long?]

C By train

The train **arriving at** platform 3 is the 16:50 train to Paris.

The Edinburgh train **departs / leaves from** platform 6. (*departs* is formal)

Is there a **restaurant car** on this train?

A: Do I have to **change trains** for Toulouse? [get off one train and get onto another]
B: No, it's a **direct** train.

D By plane

You have to **check in** two hours before the plane **takes off**. [leaves the ground]

Online check-in is also possible. / You can **check in online**.

Give your **boarding card** to the **flight attendant** when you get on the plane.

Have a good **flight**.

The plane **lands** in New York at 14:30.

After landing you have to **go through customs**.

> **Error warning**
> I went **through customs** but nobody **checked** my passport [NOT ~~controlled~~ my passport].

E By car

We **hired a car** for a week. We had to **fill** it **up with** petrol.

Can I **give** you a **lift**? I'm going into town.

(See **Unit 17: Holidays** and **Unit 47: Moving** for more useful words about travelling.)

Exercises

30.1 Match the words on the left with their definitions on the right.

1 land
2 direct
3 restaurant car
4 ship
5 timetable
6 platform
7 luggage

a a place to eat on a train
b bags and suitcases
c it says when trains depart and arrive
d you do not have to change to a different plane / train / bus
e planes do this at airports
f it travels on water, e.g. the *Titanic*
g where you stand when you are waiting for a train

30.2 Are these sentences true or false? Correct the false sentences.

1 A single ticket takes you to a place and back again. False. A return ticket takes you to a place and back again.
2 At customs, people check what you bring into the country.
3 Planes land at the beginning of a journey.
4 You need a boarding card to get off a plane.
5 Hiring a car is the same as buying a car.
6 If you give someone a lift they travel in your car.

30.3 Here are directions from the airport to John's house.

When you arrive at the airport, take a number 10 bus to the station. Then take a train to Bigtown. The journey takes half an hour and you get off the train at the second stop. Take a taxi from the station to John's house.

Now write directions from the train station to your house.

30.4 Look at the pictures and complete the crossword.

Across

3
6
7
8

Down

1
2
3
4
5

31 UK culture

A Special days

festival	date	what people do
Christmas	25th December	send Christmas cards give presents spend time with their families decorate a **Christmas tree** eat a lot
New Year's Eve / Hogmanay (Scotland)	31st December	sing and dance toast the New Year
New Year's Day	1st January	a **bank holiday** [day when most organisations are closed]
Valentine's Day	14th February	send cards to boyfriend / girlfriend / husband / wife
Easter	dates vary	give children **Easter eggs** [chocolate eggs]
Halloween	31st October	children dress up children knock at doors and ask for sweets
Bonfire Night	5th November	have a **bonfire** and **fireworks**

B Food

Traditional UK food is **fish and chips** and **roast beef and roast potatoes** [cooked in

the **oven**] with **Yorkshire pudding**. [dish made of flour, milk and eggs]

Chicken tikka masala [a kind of **curry**] comes from India, but is very popular in the UK.

C Education

type of school	what it is
nursery school	for children aged 2–4
primary school	for children aged 5–11
secondary school	for children aged 12–18
state school	parents don't pay for children to go here
private school	parents pay for children to go here

D Politics

The UK has a **royal family**, with a **king** or a **queen**.

Political decisions are made at the **Houses of Parliament**.

The **Prime Minister** is the political leader of the UK.

Exercises

31.1 Which festivals do these pictures show?

1 Halloween ....
3 ....
5 ....

2 ....
4 ....
6 ....

31.2 Look at the pictures. Find 10 more words connected with food in the puzzle.

C	H	I	C	K	E	N	F	D	K	N
R	Y	O	R	K	S	H	I	R	E	P
O	C	V	O	M	T	R	S	M	V	U
A	Q	E	W	A	A	T	H	X	L	D
S	M	V	C	S	H	G	E	Q	L	D
T	P	O	T	A	T	O	E	S	C	I
D	F	G	B	L	B	K	U	V	U	N
X	Z	O	E	A	P	I	V	Z	R	G
A	N	D	E	C	H	I	P	S	R	B
C	W	Q	F	T	I	K	K	A	Y	J

31.3 Answer these questions about traditional UK food.

1 What do British people traditionally eat with fish?   chips
2 Where does chicken tikka masala come from?
3 What is chicken tikka masala a kind of?
4 Do British people eat Yorkshire pudding after their main course?
5 In or on which part of the cooker do you make roast beef and roast potatoes?

31.4 Which kind of school do these British children go to?

1 Meena is seven. Her parents pay for her to go to school.   a private primary school
2 Alex is 14. His school is free.
3 Tim and Masha are three.
4 Mehmet is ten. His parents don't pay for him to go to school.
5 Nick is 16. His parents pay for him to go to school.

31.5 Answer these questions about politics in the UK.

1 Who is Prime Minister at the moment?
2 Where does the Prime Minister work?
3 Who is head of the royal family at the moment?

> **Tip**
>
> Learn about UK life by using the BBC Learning English website which has up-to-date articles and news stories: http://www.bbc.co.uk/worldservice/learningenglish/

32 Crime

Crimes and criminals

crime	robbery	murder /ˈmɜːdə/	burglary /ˈbɜːgləri/	mugging [attacking a person in a public place and stealing their money]
person	a robber	a murderer	a burglar	a mugger
verb	to rob somebody or a place (e.g. a bank)	to murder somebody	to break into a house / flat (break / broke / broken)	to mug somebody

crime	car theft	drug dealing	terrorism	shoplifting
person	a car thief /θiːf/	a drug dealer	a terrorist	a shoplifter
verb	to steal a car (steal / stole / stolen)	to sell drugs (sell / sold / sold)	to attack somebody or a place	to steal things from a shop

There was a **burglary** at the school last night.

John West **murdered** his wife.

There are a lot of **muggings** in the city centre.

The bank **was robbed** yesterday. My sister **was robbed** last week.

> ## Error warning
>
> A thief **steals** something (steal / stole / stolen). Somebody **stole** my bicycle. [NOT Somebody ~~robbed~~ my bicycle.]
>
> I was robbed last night. [NOT I was ~~stolen.~~]

B The law /lɔː/

A student **was arrested for** shoplifting this morning.

The **police** came to the school and spoke to his teacher.

The student has to **go to court** next week.

If he is **guilty** he will have to **pay a fine**. /ˈgɪlti/

If he is **innocent** he can go home. /ˈɪnəsənt/

I don't think he will **go to prison**.

C Other crime problems

Some **vandals** broke the windows in the telephone box.

[A vandal breaks and smashes things.]

We have a lot of **vandalism** in my town.

A lot of people **take drugs** nowadays.

Is **football hooliganism** a problem in your country? /ˈhuːlɪgənɪzm/

[A **football hooligan** is a person who goes to a football match and makes trouble.]

Exercises

32.1 **What do we call someone …**

1 who steals cars?   *a car thief*
2 who kills someone?
3 who steals things from shops?
4 who robs people's houses and flats?
5 who attacks someone in the street and steals their money?
6 who sells illegal drugs?

32.2 **Fill the gaps in these sentences.**

1 There were a lot of football h*ooligans*............... near the stadium.
2 The police officer arr............................... her for shoplifting.
3 Some van............................... destroyed all the flowers in the park.
4 He had to pay a fi............................... of £50 for parking his car in the wrong place.
5 There are a lot of bur............................... in this part of the city, so always close the windows.
6 The police made a mistake; she was inn............................... . She did not steal the money.
7 A group of terr............................... have attacked the airport.
8 He murdered his wife. He was in pr............................... for 20 years.

32.3 **True or false?**

1 A burglar goes into someone's house and steals things.   *True*
2 Vandals take people's money.
3 A murderer kills someone.
4 A car thief is someone who drives very badly or dangerously.
5 If you are guilty it means you are the person who did the crime.

32.4 **Choose the right word to complete each sentence.**

1 My brother was (robbed)/ *stolen* yesterday.
2 Someone *robbed* / *stole* my bike last night.
3 My local bank has been *robbed* / *stolen*.
4 Who has *robbed* / *stolen* my pen?
5 Someone *robbed* / *stole* our TV when we were on holiday.
6 Where were you when your keys were *robbed* / *stolen*?

Follow-up

Give your opinion. What do you think should happen to these people?

1 A man murdered his wife and three children. He should go to prison for 30 years.
2 A student with no money stole a book from a bookshop.
3 A woman sold some drugs to a teenager.
4 Some terrorists attacked a bus and killed five people.
5 A woman parked her car and blocked the traffic.
6 A teenager damaged some trees in the park.

33 The media

A Radio and TV programmes

The **news** is on TV at 6 o'clock every night. [important things that happen]

Do you watch **soaps / soap operas**? *Home and Away* is my favourite. [Soaps are stories about people's lives. They are often on TV every day.]

I like **nature programmes** best. [programmes about animals, birds, etc.]

I watched a **documentary** last night about drugs and crime. [programme looking at a social problem or question]

In **talk shows**, people talk about themselves or discuss topics with an interviewer.

The children watch **cartoons** on Saturday mornings. (For example, Disney films with animals that talk. See **Unit 22: Cinema.**)

My brother likes watching **reality TV**. [programmes that film real people living their lives, not actors]

I always watch **sports programmes**.

B Newspapers and magazines

In most countries there are **morning (news)papers** and **evening (news)papers**.

Every month, I buy a **magazine**.

My mother buys **women's magazines**.

I like **news magazines** like *Newsweek* and *Time*.

In most magazines and newspapers there are lots of **adverts / advertisements**. [something that tries to persuade people to buy something]

Other types of magazines: **sports magazines / computer magazines / teenage magazines**. (See **Unit 23: Free time at home.**)

C People and the media

There was **an interview with** the US President on TV last night.

The **reporters** are outside Zelda Glitzberg's house. [people who go out and get the news stories where they happen]

My sister is a **journalist**; she writes for *The Oxford Times* newspaper. [person who writes articles]

D Expressions

You can **read newspapers** or **watch TV online**.

What's your **favourite TV programme**?

What's on TV tonight?

Is it OK if I **change the channel**?

> ### Error warning
> The news **is** on now. [NOT The news ~~are~~ on now.]

Exercises

33.1 Fill the gaps in these sentences.

1 Ten million people watch this ...programme........ every week. It's very popular.
2 The news .... on channel 3 at 9 o'clock every night.
3 There was a .... about traffic problems in cities on TV last night.
4 I saw a .... programme about birds in Antarctica.
5 My sister is 13; she reads a .... magazine every week. She likes the stories about boys.
6 With my computer I can read the sports news ....
7 I'd like to watch the news now. Is it OK if I .... the channel?
8 Did you see the .... with the Prime Minister last night?

33.2 Match the left-hand column with the type of programme on the right.

1 Talking about family problems   a International news
2 Film of elephants in Africa   b Sports programme
3 Football cup final   c Reality TV programme
4 Reports from all over the world   d Soap (opera)
5 Maria decides not to marry Philip   e Nature programme
6 Ten people in a house – they cannot   f Talk show
   leave or talk to anyone outside

33.3 What do you call ...

1 a person who goes out and gets stories for newspapers?   *a reporter*
2 a person who writes articles in newspapers and magazines?
3 a newspaper you can buy every day after about 5 pm?
4 a programme with stories made from lots of pictures?
5 a programme on TV about animals, birds, etc?
6 something in a magazine or on TV that tries to sell something?
7 something like CNN or Sky Sports?
8 a meeting when a reporter asks a person questions for TV or a newspaper?

33.4 Answer these questions for yourself.

1 Do you read a morning or an evening newspaper?
2 What kinds of magazine do you read?
3 What will you watch on TV tonight?
4 What is your favourite TV channel?
5 How many hours of TV do you watch every day?
6 What are your favourite kinds of TV programmes?
7 Do you ever watch TV online?
8 Do you like watching adverts on TV?

Follow-up

Go to http://www.bbc.co.uk/ Listen to radio programmes and download podcasts that interest you.

34 Problems at home and work

A At home

The TV **isn't working**. Can you **repair** it?

The washing machine is **broken**.
We need to **mend** it.

The plants **are dying**.
Did you forget to **water** them?

The room is **untidy**. We must **tidy** it.

I've **lost** my keys. Will you help me **look for** them?

You've **cut** your finger.
You should **put on a plaster**.

You've **had a row** /raʊ/ **with** a friend. Will you **apologise**? [say 'I'm sorry']

B At work

Carla **had a bad day** at work yesterday. She was **late for** work.

She had **too much work** to do.

Her colleague was **in a bad mood**.

Her **computer crashed**.

The photocopier was **out of order**.

The coffee machine **wasn't working**.

Tip

When you need to make a list of things to do,
make it in English, e.g.

Mend my bike   Water the plants
Tidy my desk

Exercises

34.1 Look at the pictures. What is the problem?

1   3   5   7

2   4   6   8

1 The coffee machine isn't working.
2 ....
3 ....
4 ....
5 ....
6 ....
7 ....
8 ....

34.2 Write down three nouns that can go with these words:

1 broken window / cup / glass ....
2 cut ....
3 untidy ....
4 late for ....
5 a .... that isn't working
6 too much ....

34.3 Have you ever had these problems? Number each one 0–3 (0 = never, 1 = once or twice,
2 = quite often, 3 = frequently).

1 a TV that doesn't work 2   7 a broken washing machine
2 dying plants   8 an untidy bedroom
3 a cut finger   9 a row with a friend
4 being late for work or school   10 your computer crashes
5 a colleague or friend in a bad mood 11 lost keys
6 a coffee machine that isn't working 12 too much work

34.4 Look at Carla's problems in B. What could she do?

She was late for work – get a new alarm clock.

34.5 Can you think of four problems that you or a friend have had recently? Write them down
in English. Use a dictionary to help you.

....
....

35 Global problems

A Natural disasters

There was a **hurricane / snowstorm / forest fire** there last year.

hurricane [a very strong wind]

snowstorm [a lot of snow and wind at the same time]

forest fire [when it is very dry and trees catch fire]

San Francisco has had a lot of **earthquakes.** [when the earth moves]

There were serious **floods** in the north yesterday. [too much water]

The river often **floods** after heavy rain. [water goes over the river banks]

B Man-made problems

There are too many people in some places. Cities are too **crowded.**

Many people are:

poor [they do not have enough money]

hungry [they do not have enough food]

homeless [they do not have a place to live]

unemployed [they do not have a job]

There is a lot of **pollution** in many places. [when the air, water or earth is dirty and bad for people, plants and animals]

The river is **polluted** and a lot of fish have died.

The **air pollution** is very bad today.

The American **War** of Independence started in 1775 and ended in 1783. [fighting between two or more countries or nationalities] It lasted for eight years.

The teachers are **on strike** today. [when people refuse to work because, for example, they want more money]

He had a **car crash** on the way to work.

The **traffic jams** in the city are terrible in the **rush hour**. [times when everyone is going to work]

Exercises

35.1 What problems can you see in the pictures?

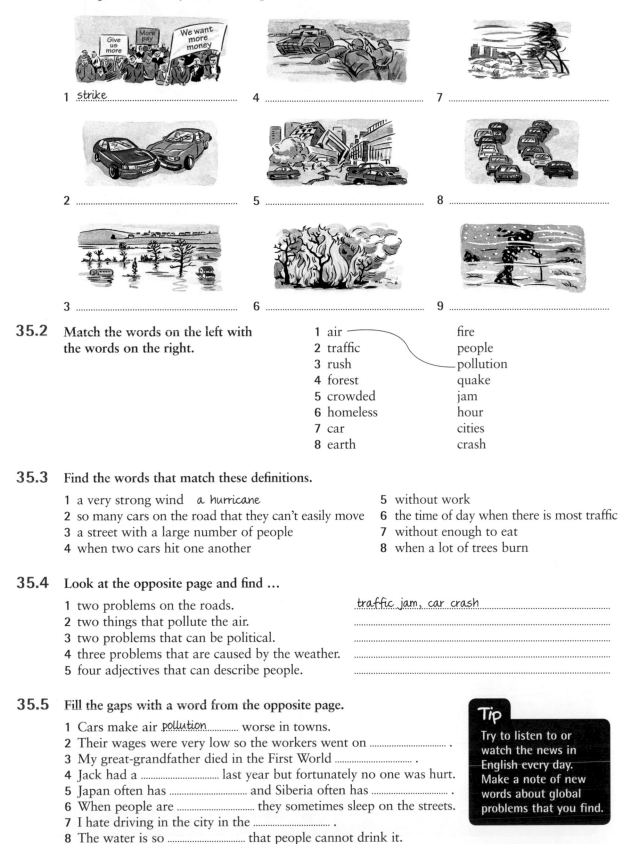

1 strike ....

4 ....

7 ....

2 ....

5 ....

8 ....

3 ....

6 ....

9 ....

35.2 Match the words on the left with the words on the right.

1 air	fire
2 traffic	people
3 rush	pollution
4 forest	quake
5 crowded	jam
6 homeless	hour
7 car	cities
8 earth	crash

35.3 Find the words that match these definitions.

1 a very strong wind   a hurricane
2 so many cars on the road that they can't easily move
3 a street with a large number of people
4 when two cars hit one another

5 without work
6 the time of day when there is most traffic
7 without enough to eat
8 when a lot of trees burn

35.4 Look at the opposite page and find ...

1 two problems on the roads.   traffic jam, car crash ....
2 two things that pollute the air.   ....
3 two problems that can be political.   ....
4 three problems that are caused by the weather.   ....
5 four adjectives that can describe people.   ....

35.5 Fill the gaps with a word from the opposite page.

1 Cars make air pollution............ worse in towns.
2 Their wages were very low so the workers went on ....
3 My great-grandfather died in the First World ....
4 Jack had a .... last year but fortunately no one was hurt.
5 Japan often has .... and Siberia often has ....
6 When people are .... they sometimes sleep on the streets.
7 I hate driving in the city in the ....
8 The water is so .... that people cannot drink it.

Tip

Try to listen to or watch the news in English every day. Make a note of new words about global problems that you find.

36 Have / had / had

A What can you have?

You can ...

    have breakfast **lunch** **dinner** **a meal**

    have a party **a meeting** **a game** (of football, etc.)

    have a lesson **an exam** **homework**

    have a cup of tea / coffee **a drink** **an ice cream** **some cheese**

    have a shower /'ʃaʊə/ **a bath** **a swim**

B Expressions with have

Is that your camera? Can I **have a look**? [look at it]

Is that your bicycle? Can I **have a go**? [ride it]

Goodbye! **Have a good journey!** [somebody is going away]

Do you **have a moment**? [have some time] Can I **have a word with** you? [speak to you]

We always **have a good time** in our English lessons [fun; we enjoy them]

I'm going to **have my hair cut**. See you later. Can you meet me at the hairdresser's?

I want to learn to ski but I **don't have the time**.

C Have + got (speaking / informal) = have (writing / formal)

I've **got** three sisters. **Have** you **got** any brothers and sisters?

My house is big. **It's got** five bedrooms and three bathrooms.

We've got ten minutes before the train goes.

Have you **got** a pen?

(*in a shop*) A: Do you sell postcards? B: Yes, but we **haven't got** any at the moment.

I've **got** a problem. Can I have a word with you?

I've got a cold / a headache. /'hedeɪk/

D Have got to (speaking / informal) = have to (writing / formal)

We use **have (got) to** when the situation means you are obliged to do something.

The museum's not free. You **have to / you've got to** pay $10 to go in.

All students **have to do** an exam.

My sister needs the car, so **I've got to** walk to school every day this week.

> ### Error warning
> In the past, we use **had to**, without 'got'. When I was a student, I **had to** write an essay every week [NOT I had ~~got~~ to write an essay].

> ### Tip
> Group expressions together which belong to the same topic, for example, **have** + words for meals (*breakfast, lunch, dinner*), **have** + 'study' words (*an exam, a test, a lesson, a class*), etc.

Exercises

36.1 Fill the gaps in the sentences. Use words from A and B opposite.

1 I always have coffee in the morning.
2 I have a tennis .... every Saturday morning. My teacher is excellent.
3 Do you want to have a game of .... ?
4 Jane's having a .... on Saturday. Are you going?
5 Do you want to have a .... ? The bathroom's just here.
6 I have an .... tomorrow, so I have to study tonight.
7 We must have a .... to talk about these problems.
8 I'm going to the cafeteria to have a .... Do you want to come?
9 The hotel has a swimming pool, so we can have a .... every day.
10 We can have .... before the film, or we can eat after it.

36.2 Correct the mistakes.

1 Please phone Grandma when you have ~~the~~ moment.   *a*
2 Nadia has gone to the hairdresser's to have cut her hair.
3 That computer game looks great. Can I have a going?
4 I want to have some words with my teacher after the lesson.
5 Mum didn't have the times to go to the shop today.
6 They don't have got any cake in the café today.

36.3 Complete the crossword.

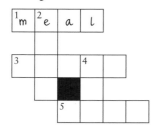

Across

1 You have it in a restaurant.
3 People often have one on their birthday.
5 Do you want to have a .... of tennis?

Down

2 You have it at school or university.
4 If you don't like coffee, you can have ....

36.4 What do you say?

1 (*someone is thirsty*) Why don't you have a drink ?
2 (*someone is going away*) Bye! Have a .... !
3 (*someone sneezes [Atishoo!] and has a red nose*) Oh! Have you got a .... ?
4 (*someone has a new camera*) Is that new? Can I have a .... ?

36.5 Answer the questions.

1 Have you got any brothers or sisters?
2 What time do you have English lessons?
3 What do you have for lunch?
4 Do you have to go to lessons every day?
5 How many pens have you got with you now?
6 Do you always have a good time in your English classes?

37 Go / went / gone

A Go

Go means to move from one place to another.

I **go** to work **by** bike. My brother **goes by** car.

We **went** to Paris last summer.

Is this train **going** to Granada?

Shall we **go** to the
swimming pool today?

Where **does** this road **go**?

B Go + prepositions

Kim **went in**(to) his room
and shut the door.

Yuko **went out of** the house
and **into** the garden.

Arthur was tired. He **went
up** the stairs slowly.

The phone was ringing. She
went down the stairs quickly.

C Future plans

Be going to is often used to talk about future plans.

Jan is **going to study** maths at university.

We're **going to visit** my aunt in New York soon.

I'm **going to learn** five new words every day.

D Expressions Go + *-ing* for activities

Go is often used with *-ing* for different activities.

I hate **going shopping**.

I usually **go swimming**
in the morning.

Let's **go dancing**.

Do you like **going sightseeing**
when you are on holiday?

Hans **goes skiing**
every winter.

Bob is **going
fishing** today.

Error warning

Let's **go swimming** and then **go shopping**. [NOT Let's ~~go to / for swimming~~ and then ~~go to / for shopping~~.]

I **go there** every week. I don't want to **go anywhere / somewhere** else. [NOT I ~~go to there~~ every week. I don't want to ~~go to anywhere / somewhere~~ else.]

I must **go home** at 10 o'clock. [NOT I must ~~go to / at home~~ at 10 o'clock.]

Exercises

37.1 Where are these people going? Follow the lines.

1 Pablo *is going to the zoo.* ....
2 The Sharps ....
3 Lili and Karl ....
4 Imran ....
5 Jan ....

37.2 Write about Alison's New Year Resolutions.

This year I'm going to:

stop eating chocolate

pass my driving test

learn Spanish

watch less TV

keep my room tidy

1 This year *Alison is going to stop eating chocolate.*
2 This year ....
3 This year ....
4 This year ....
5 This year ....

37.3 Look at the activities in D opposite. Which do you do on holiday? Write sentences.

I usually go shopping on holiday.

37.4 Where do trains, buses and roads go to from your town?

From Cambridge, trains go to London and to Norwich.

37.5 Are these sentences correct? If not, correct them.

1 It's time to go at home now.
   X   It's time to go home now.
2 Mum is going for shopping this afternoon.
3 I'm going to London by car tomorrow.
4 I love Paris. Did you go to there last year?
5 Milos is going to home at 4 o'clock.
6 We always go to the same café. Let's go
   to somewhere different today.
7 Excuse me, please. Where does this bus go?

8 I go to swimming every Sunday
   morning.
9 We're going sightsee today.
10 Jo went down to the top of the hill.
11 Let's go to fish today.
12 She went out off the shop.
13 Please go away. I'm tired.
14 Would you like to go to home now?

Follow-up

Look in an English story book. Find five examples of *go.*
Write them down in your vocabulary notebook.

38 Do / did / done

A Do as auxiliary

questions	**Do** you **like** tennis?	**Did** they **like** the film?
short answers	Yes, I **do**.	Yes, they **did**.
	So **does** Sinjit.	So **did** I.
negatives	He **doesn't play** well.	Jo **didn't see** it.

B What are you doing?

Do as a general verb:

On Saturdays I usually **do** nothing. I just relax.

Don't do that, Tommy.

What **are** the people in the picture **doing**?

They're dancing.

C What do you do?

A: What **do** you **do**? (= What is your job?)
B: I'm a student. / I'm a secretary.

A: What **does** your wife **do**? (= What's your wife's job?)
B: She's a doctor. / She's a teacher.

(See **Unit 14: Jobs.**)

D Do + activity

do the housework

do the gardening

do the washing

do the washing-up

do your homework

do some exercises

do business with

do your best

A: Did you **do the washing** this morning?
B: No, I'm going to **do** it later.

Our company **does a lot of business with** the US.

The homework is very difficult – just **do your best**.

> ### Tip
> Make a note of any expressions with do that you find when you are reading in English.
> See Unit 39 for the contrast between *do* and *make*.

Exercises

38.1 Write questions and answers about the people in the picture.

1 (the boy) What is the boy doing? He's eating an ice cream. ....
2 (the girls) ....
3 (the dog) ....
4 (the man in the house) ....
5 (the woman) ....
6 (the man in the garden) ....

38.2 Write questions and answers about the jobs of the people in the pictures.

1 Lee Atkins   2 Lara Brown   2 Sophie Hicks   4 Jo and Ted

1 What does Lee Atkins do? He's a teacher. ....
2 ....
3 ....
4 ....

38.3 Write questions about what the people in Exercise 38.2 did this morning. Answer the questions using the correct form of the phrases in the box.

| talk to five patients   ~~teach three lessons~~   write an essay   go to a meeting |

1 What did Lee Atkins do? He taught three lessons. ....
2 ....
3 ....
4 ....

38.4 Look at the *do* expressions in D. Write sentences using these activities.

I do a lot of housework but I never do the gardening.

38.5 Correct the mistakes in this dialogue.

ANNA: Where did you ~~went~~ on your holidays? To London?   go
PAVEL: No, we don't go to London this year. We went to Scotland.
ANNA: Do your grandmother lives in Scotland?
PAVEL: No, she don't but my uncle do.

39 Make / made / made

A Make ...

Dad is **making some coffee.**   Mum is **making dinner.**

I'll **make some tea / hot chocolate.** /'tʃɒklət/
I **make breakfast / lunch / dinner** every day.

He's **making a photocopy.**   She's **making a film / video.**

B It makes me (feel) ...

Going by train always **makes me (feel)** tired.
My friend called me stupid. It **made me (feel)** angry.
That film **made me (feel)** sad.

C Expressions

You use **make** NOT ~~do~~ in these expressions:

I **made a mistake** in the exercise.

I want to **make an appointment** with the doctor. [fix a time to see him/her]

When I get up I **make my bed.**

The children are **making a noise.**

Yes, and they are **making a mess** in the living room!

I love your new dress – you **made a** good **choice.**

> ### Error warning
> You **do homework** [NOT ~~make homework~~]. You **take** or **do an exam** [NOT ~~make an exam~~].
> You **take a photo** [NOT ~~make a photo~~]. You **do the washing** [NOT ~~make the washing~~].

Exercises

39.1 Complete the sentences with the correct form of *make*.

1 I always _make_ a lot of mistakes when I speak English.
2 Our neighbours had a party last night. They .... a lot of noise.
3 I am .... dinner for my parents this evening.
4 What do you think, the silver car or the white one? We must .... our choice today.
5 I .... an appointment with the doctor for you. It's at 5 o'clock.
6 Craig is in the kitchen. He is .... a cup of tea.

39.2 Complete the sentences with *make(s) / made me feel* + an adjective from the box.

sick	tired	~~sad~~	happy	angry

1 That film about the war _made me feel sad_ .
2 Long lessons always ....
3 She was horrible to me; it ....
4 It's a lovely song. It ....
5 That meal was horrible. It ....

39.3 What are these people doing? Complete the sentences using *make*.

1 He's _making a photocopy_

3 The children are ....
....

5 The children are ....
....

2 She's ....
....

4 They're ....
....

6 The girl is ....
....

39.4 Correct the mistakes in these sentences.

1 I have to ~~make~~ my homework.   _I have to do my homework._
2 Can I make a photo of you?
3 He's 25 but he never makes his own washing. He takes his dirty clothes to his mother's.
4 Are you making an exam tomorrow?
5 Have you made your homework yet?

> **Follow-up**
>
> Make a page for expressions with *make* and *do* in your vocabulary notebook. Make two
> columns – one with the heading *make* and the other with the heading *do*. Write down all the
> *make* and *do* expressions you know in the appropriate columns. Add new expressions to the
> page as you meet them.

40 Come / came / come

Come and go are different:

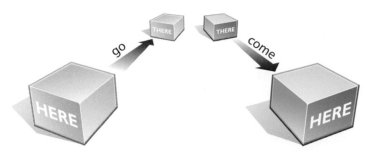

A · Come in / out

We say 'Come in!' when someone knocks at the door of a room.

Then the person who knocked comes into the room.

Come out (of) is often the opposite of come in (to).

A woman came out of the shop with two big bags. (I was in the street.)

You put your money in and the ticket comes out of the machine.

B · Come back and come home

Come back means 'return to this place here'.

She went away for three days. She came back yesterday. (She is here again.)

Come back is often used with from.

They came back from Italy yesterday.

Come home is similar; 'home' is 'here' for the person speaking.

MUM: What time did you come home last night?
ANNE: Oh, about 3 o'clock.
MUM: What! That's much too late!

C · Other important uses of come

A: What country do you come from?
B: I'm from Poland. / I come from Poland. / I'm Polish.

We're going clubbing tonight. Do you want to come along? [come with us]

Come and see me some time. [visit me]

Error warning

I come from Poland [NOT I'm coming from Poland].

Tip

Write down any prepositions you find with *come* every time you see them.

Exercises

40.1 Fill the gaps in the sentences.

1 I put money in, but the ticket didn't come _out of_ the machine.
2 A: I'm going to Thailand tomorrow.
  B: Oh! When are you coming .... ?
  A: In two weeks.
3 The teacher came .... the classroom and started the lesson.
4 A: Where do you come .... ?
  B: I'm Spanish.
5 Come and .... me at 5 o'clock; we can talk about it then.
6 The children come .... school at 4 o'clock.

40.2 What do you think these people are saying? Use words from the box.

come from	~~come in~~	come along	come here

1 _Come in!_ ....

3 ....

2 ....

4 ....

40.3 Fill the gaps using *come* in the correct form.

1 Did you _come_ for your letters? They're on the table.
2 She .... back yesterday.
3 He .... here every Tuesday.
4 .... you .... to the party tonight?
5 Daljit .... from a small town in India.

40.4 Answer these questions for yourself.

1 What time do you come home every day?
2 What country do you come from?
3 What do you do when you come into your classroom?

Follow-up

Look up these verbs in a dictionary. Write down the meaning and one example for each verb. After a week, cover the verbs and examples, look at the meanings and see if you can remember the verbs.

Verb	Meaning	Example
come round	....	....
come across	....	....
come up	....	....

A Take with time (it + take + person + time)

It **takes** Alan 20 minutes to get to work.

Alan's house → 20 minutes → Alan's office

It **takes** Miriam 45 minutes to get to work.

Miriam's flat → 45 minutes → Miriam's office

I go to school / university every day. It **takes** me 30 minutes.

I do homework every day. It **took** /tʊk/ me two hours yesterday.

How long does it take to get to the station? Fifteen minutes in a taxi.

How long did it take you to learn the Greek alphabet? A week or two.

B Take something with you

Are you going out? **Take** an umbrella. It's raining.

Are you going to the beach? **Take** some water with you.

Sorry, you can't **take** your camera into the museum.

C Expressions

Can I **take a photo / photograph** here? /ˈfəʊtəʊ/ /ˈfəʊtəgræf/

A: Are you **taking an** English **course**? B: Yes.

A: Do you have to **take an exam**? B: Yes, at the end of the course.

I want to **take some** Japanese **lessons**.

How do you get to work? I **take the bus**.

In London you can **take the underground** to the London Eye.

We **took a taxi** from the airport to our hotel.

How does Nick get to work? He **takes the train**.

> **Tip**
>
> Make a page in your notebook for *take* and put in new words that go with it when you see them (e.g. *take a picture, take a look at, take a chance*).

Exercises

41.1 Fill the gaps for yourself.

1 It _takes_ me .... minutes to get to school / university / work.
2 It takes me .... minutes to go from my house to the nearest railway station.
3 It takes me .... minutes to get to my best friend's house.
4 .... takes me .... to do one unit of this book.

41.2 Complete the sentences using *take* and an expression from the box.

| a course   some water   the train   ~~an exam~~ |

1 At the end of the course, you have to   _take an exam._ ....
2 You can fly from London to Paris or you can   ....
3 You want to learn Russian? Why don't you   .... ?
4 If you go out on a hot day, you need to   ....

41.3 Look at the pictures. Answer the questions using *take*.

1 How does Lisa go to work?
She takes the train. ....

3 How does Simon go to school?
He ....

2 How can I get to the airport?
You ....

4 How do Paulo and Anna get home every day?
They ....

41.4 What do you take with you when ...

1 you want to take photographs?   _I take my camera._
2 it's raining?
3 you go to another country?
4 you go to your English lessons?
5 you need to text someone?

41.5 How long did it take you to do this unit?

42 Bring / brought / brought

A Bring and take

take (like go) = from *here* to *there*
bring (like come) = from *there* to *here*

Are you going to school? **Take** your books. (= *from here* to the school)

Are you going to the kitchen? Can you **bring** me a glass? (= from the kitchen *to here*)

Please **take** this form to the secretary. (= the secretary is *there*)

Come to my house tomorrow and **bring** your guitar. (= for me, my house is *here*)

B Bring somebody something

A: I've **brought** /brɔːt/ you some apples from my garden. B: Oh, thank you!

When she visits me, she always **brings** me flowers.

C Bring something back

It's raining. You can take my umbrella and **bring** it **back** tomorrow.

TOM: This book is interesting.
ANN: Please **take** it with you and read it.
TOM: Thanks. I'll **bring** it **back** on Friday.
ANN: OK. No problem.

Exercises

42.1 Fill the gaps with *bring* or *take*.

1 Are you going to the shops? _Take_ an umbrella. It's raining.
2 'Don't forget to .... your books tomorrow!' the teacher said to the class.
3 Are you going to the kitchen? Can you .... me some water?
4 .... your camera with you when you go to Thailand. It's beautiful there.
5 Are you going to the office? Can you .... these papers, please?
6 I'll .... you a present from New York.

42.2 Match the words on the left with the words on the right.

1 Yesterday he brought me   a these letters, please.
2 You must take   b bring your guitar.
3 Come to my house and   c some flowers.
4 Go to the post office and take   d food to the party.
5 Everybody is going to bring   e your passport when you travel.

42.3 Fill the gaps with the correct form of *bring* or *take*.

1 She always _brings_ me presents. Yesterday she .... me some chocolates.
2 Hello, I've .... you some flowers. I hope you like them!
3 Can you .... this present when you go and see Sonia?
4 She is going to .... my book, read it tonight and .... it back tomorrow.

42.4 Fill the gaps with *bring back* or *take*.

1 Can I _take_ this magazine to read tonight? I'll .... it ....
tomorrow.
2 When she went to Belgium, she .... me .... some chocolates.
3 Please .... my umbrella. You can .... it .... tomorrow.

42.5 Where are you now?
If you are at an English lesson now, answer a).
If you are not at an English lesson, answer b).

a Name three things you always bring to the lesson.
b Name three things you always take to the lesson.

43 Get / got / got

A Get with adjectives: for changes

It's light. ⟶ It's **getting** dark. ⟶ It's dark.

She's ill. ⟶ She's **getting** better. ⟶ She's better. / She's well.

I'm **getting** tired. I want to go to bed.

It's raining! I'm **getting** wet!

B Get with nouns

If you **don't have** something you can **get** it. [get = buy or find]

I want to send a postcard. I have to **get** a stamp.

I'm going to the shop to **get** a newspaper.

Do you want a drink? I can **get** some coffee.

Where can I **get** a taxi?

I've finished my studies. Now I want to **get** a job.

My friend is ill! Please **get** a doctor.

C Expressions

Maria and David are **getting married** in April.

A: When you **get to** New York, call me. [arrive at, reach] B: OK, give me your number.

A: How can I **get to** the airport? B: Take the airport bus at the bus station.

I'll see you when you **get back** from Hong Kong. [return, come home]

(See also **get up** in Unit 45.)

> ### Error warning
>
> When I **get home**, I have my lunch [NOT When I get ~~to~~ home].
> I **get there** at 6 o'clock, so please ring me at 6.30 [NOT I get ~~to~~ there].

Exercises

43.1 Complete these sentences using a, b or c.

1 I studied too much and I got   a) hot   (b) tired   c) sick.
2 I ate too much and I got   a) hot   b) tired   c) sick.
3 I sat in the sun too much and I got   a) hot   b) tired   c) sick.
4 In winter in the north it gets   a) tired   b) dark   c) wet   very early.
5 Ahmed got very   a) dark   b) better   c) wet   in the rain.

43.2 Complete these sentences using the correct form of *get* and a word from the box.

> better   light   ~~dark~~   cold   wet

1 The sun is going down. It's ...getting dark...
2 When the sun comes up it ....
3 She's in hospital but she ....
4 It's raining! I .... !
5 Please close the window. I ....

43.3 What / Who do you get if ...

1 you want to post a letter?   a stamp
2 somebody is ill?
3 you are thirsty?
4 you want to write something down?
5 you want to read the news?
6 you want to go to the airport?
7 you want to earn some money?
8 you want to go out and it's raining?

43.4 Complete these sentences.

Singapore (dep. 05.45)   Paris (arr. 12.30)

1 This plane ...gets to.............. Paris at 12.30.

university   (25 minutes)   my house

2 The bus from the university .... my house in 25 minutes.

3 When does the flight from Moscow .... London?
4 José usually leaves work at 6 and .... home at 6.30.
5 Mike is in New York. He won't .... till the 14th July.

43.5 Answer the questions. Write sentences.

1 In your country, how old are people usually when they get married?
2 When do people usually get married? Which day? Which month(s)?
3 What time do you usually get home every day? How do you get there?

Phrasal verbs

A What are phrasal verbs?

Phrasal verbs have two parts: a verb + a particle.

get up / on / off

I **got up** at 6.30 this morning. I'm tired now.

We should **get on** the bus. It's leaving in five minutes!

We **got off** the bus at the City Museum.

turn on / off / up / down

He always **turns on** the TV at 9 o'clock to watch the news.

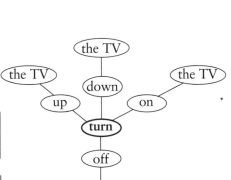

It's a sunny day. **Turn** the light **off**.

Turn the TV **up**. I can't hear it.

Turn the TV **down**. It's too loud.

go on / off

Don't stop. **Go on** talking. It's very interesting. [continue]

Karen **went off** and forgot her handbag. [left]

put something on

It's cold and windy outside. **Put** your coat **on**. / **Put on** your coat.

come on

Come on! We're late.

B One phrasal verb, different meanings

Note that one phrasal verb can often have different meanings.

turn down

She **turned down** the stereo. [made it not so loud]

She **turned down** the invitation. [refused it]

take off

Our plane **takes off** at 12.30. [leaves the ground]

She **took off** her shoes. [removed them from her feet]

> **Tip**
>
> Make a special page in your notebook. Write down any phrasal verbs you see or hear. Organise them into groups, in any way that makes sense to you, for example, clothes, movement.

Exercises

44.1 Match a sentence on the left with a sentence on the right.

1 It's eight o'clock.   a I'm going to turn it down.
2 We arrived at our station.   b Please turn your music down.
3 That funny programme is on soon.   c It's time to get up.
4 The bus arrived.   d We got off the train.
5 I'm trying to work.   e Put on your raincoat.
6 I can't hear the news.   f We got on.
7 It's raining today.   g Turn on the TV.
8 I don't want to accept that job.   h Turn the radio up.

44.2 Put the correct prepositions in these sentences.

1 It's dark in here. Turn ..on............................ the lights.
2 Our plane takes .... at 6.25 and lands at 7.50.
3 Come .... ! It's time to get .... You'll be late for school!
4 The children took .... their school uniforms when they got home.
5 It's time to turn .... the TV and go to bed now.
6 Get .... the bus at the train station, then walk about 100 metres and you'll see the theatre.
7 The students went .... working until late at night.
8 When they got to the beach, he put .... his swimming trunks and ran down to the sea.

44.3 What is happening in these pictures? Use one of the phrasal verbs from the opposite page to describe each picture.

1 _They are getting on the coach._

3 ....

2 ....

4 .... oven.

44.4 Replace the underlined words with a phrasal verb from the opposite page.

1 The plane <u>left</u> at midnight. _The plane took off at midnight._
2 I <u>removed</u> my hat and coat.
3 She <u>continued</u> writing novels all her life.
4 Michael <u>left</u> without saying goodbye to anybody.
5 I <u>refused</u> the invitation to Maya's wedding.

45 Everyday things

A Things we do every day

I wake up

get up

go to the bathroom

have a shower

have breakfast /'brekfəst/

listen to the radio /'lɪsən/

go to work

come home

make dinner

phone (or call) a friend

watch TV

go to bed

B Sometimes I ...

wash clothes

clean the house

go for a walk

write letters / emails

C Expressions

A: **How often do you** read the newspaper / watch TV?
B: Three or four times a week.

A: **What time do you** get up / go to work?
B: At 7 o'clock normally.

A: **How do you** go to work?
B: Usually by bus / train / car.

Error warning

We say **I usually get up at 8 o'clock**, but today **I got up at 8.30**. [NOT ~~I used to /~~ ~~I'm used to get up~~ at 8 o'clock.]

(See also **Unit 36: Have / had / had** and **Unit 39: Make / made / made**.)

Exercises

45.1 What do they usually do?

1 <u>He listens to the radio every morning.</u>

2 She w... (every Saturday)

3 He c.. (every weekend)

4 He w.. (every evening)

5 She g.. (every Sunday)

45.2 Ask questions.

topic	question	answer
1 get up	What time do you get up?	7.30, usually.
2 go for a walk	How …	Every Saturday.
3 go to work	How …	By train.
4 have dinner	When …	At about 7 o'clock usually.
5 come home from work	How …	I normally walk home.
6 phone your best friend	How …	Two or three times a week.
7 clean your room	When …	On Saturday morning usually.
8 have a shower	What …	Usually at about 11 pm.

45.3 Complete the sentences about yourself.

1 I usually wake up at ....
2 I go to the bathroom and have ....
3 I usually have .... for breakfast.
4 I go to work by ....
5 I usually have a cup of tea / coffee at .... o'clock.
6 I usually come home at ....
7 I usually .... dinner at .... o'clock.
8 In the evenings I normally .... or ....
9 Sometimes I .... a letter or email or .... to the radio.
10 I usually .... to bed at ....

A Say (say / said / said)

We use **say** when we report someone's words.

She **said**, 'This is horrible!'

He **said that** he wanted a drink.

We **say hello / goodbye** and we **say please / thank you / Happy Birthday / Merry Christmas / Happy New Year / Congratulations!** /kəngrætʃəˈleɪʃnz/

How do you say 'book' in Spanish?

Libro

We use **say** when we ask about language.

B Tell (tell / told / told)

Tell is usually followed immediately by a person. **Say** is not followed immediately by a person.

Tell is often used with *how* and *wh*-words (when, what, why, where) to find out and give information.

Tell me when you want to have dinner. She **told me how** to send a text message.

You can **tell someone the time / a story / a joke / your name / address / phone number.**

Error warning

He **told me** his name. [NOT He ~~said me~~ his name.]

Error warning

Can you **tell me** where the bus station is, please? [NOT Can you ~~say me~~ ... ?]

C Ask

Ask is used for questions.

My sister **asked me** where I was going. / My sister **asked (me)**, 'Where are you going?'

A: Can I **ask you a question**?
B: Yes.
A: What day of the week were you born?
B: Thursday.

You can **ask someone the way / the time.**

You can **ask somebody to do something** and **ask someone for something.**

I asked him to turn off his radio. (*or* I said, 'Please turn off your radio.')

She **asked for** the bill. (*or* She said, 'Can I have the bill, please?')

D Speak / talk / answer / reply

I like **talking to** you. [having a conversation with you]

Error warning

Do you **speak** Japanese? (used for languages) [NOT Do you ~~talk~~ Japanese?]

Can you **answer** the telephone / the door, please? [pick up the phone / open the door to see who it is]

Teacher: Who can **answer** the next question? Joanna?

He didn't **reply to** my email. (also used for letters / faxes / texts) [he did not send me an email back]

Exercises

46.1 **Fill the gaps with the correct form of *say* or *tell*.**

1 Can you _tell_ me where the Plaza Hotel is, please?
2 She .... me her name.
3 I .... goodbye to her.
4 'Please .... me a story,' the little boy ....
5 'Come here!' the police officer ....
6 The teacher .... her students that they were very good.

46.2 **What do you say?**

1 You want to know if an English friend can help you talk to a Russian person who does not know English.
Can _you speak Russian?_ ....
2 You want to know the word for 'tree' in German.
How ....
3 You want to know the time.
Excuse me, can you ....
4 Your course is finished. You want to say goodbye to your teacher.
I just want to ....
5 You want to know when the exam is.
Can you ....
6 The telephone rings. You are busy cooking food. A friend is watching you.
(*to your friend*)
Can you ....

46.3 **Match the verbs on the left with the words on the right.**

1 say ——————————
2 answer
3 ask for
4 reply to ——————
5 tell
6 talk to
7 ask
8 speak

a a letter
b someone to help you
c Japanese
d Happy New Year
e a friend
f someone a joke
g the bill
h the door

46.4 **Complete the phrases.**

1 (*on December 24th or 25th*) _Happy_ .... Christmas!
2 (*you want to pay in a restaurant*) Can we have .... , please?
3 (*on the first day of the year*) .... Year!
4 (*small child to parent*) .... a story before I go to sleep. Please!

47 Moving

A Without transport

walk   run   jump   dance   swim   climb   fall

When talking about the past, we say: walked / ran / jumped / danced / swam / climbed / fell.

B Transport

verb	transport	example
go by	car / plane / bus / train / bike / motorbike / ship / taxi / underground [NOT by ~~a~~ car]	We **went** to Paris **by** train last summer.
take	a / the bus / train / plane / a taxi / the underground	I **took** a taxi home yesterday.
ride	a bicycle / bike / motorbike / horse	I always **rode** my bike to school.
drive	a car / bus / train	My uncle **drove** a bus for ten years.

The pilot **flies** a plane.

How did you get to Istanbul? We **flew** there.

Error warning

You **arrive at** or **in** a place [NOT ~~arrive to~~ a place]. The train **arrived in** Tokyo on time. The plane **arrived** late **at** Heathrow.

C Expressions

Please pass the salt.

Can I help you carry your luggage?

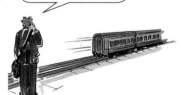

I've just missed the train.

If we don't leave now we won't catch our train.

Tip

When you are travelling you will probably see a lot of signs and information in English. Make a note of any new words and expressions you see.

(See Unit 30: Travelling.)

Exercises

47.1 Complete the sentences using verbs from A opposite. Write them in the correct form.

1 Jack likes _running_ round the park every morning but Silvia prefers _walking_ round it with her dog.
2 Everyone .... at the party last night.
3 Every day Jane .... ten lengths of the pool before breakfast.
4 James can .... very fast. He has won a lot of races.
5 Robert loves .... mountains.
6 The old lady .... on her way home and broke her arm.
7 Sandra .... into the swimming pool and quickly .... to the other side.
8 It is better for you to .... to work than to go by car.

47.2 *Ride, drive, go by* or *take*? Write the correct word(s) in the sentence.

1 Can you _ride_ a motorbike?
2 He works for a railway company. He .... a train.
3 She sometimes .... the underground to work.
4 He goes away from home a lot. He .... a lorry.
5 I prefer to .... a bus than .... car.
6 Would you like to .... an elephant?
7 You never forget how to .... a bicycle.
8 I usually .... a taxi when it rains.

47.3 Complete the diagram with six possible words.

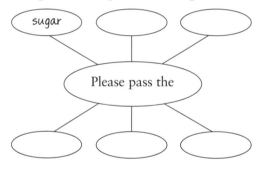

47.4 Put these sentences into the past tense with the word *yesterday*.

1 Laura runs a mile every day.   She ran a mile yesterday.
2 Maria often drives her grandmother to the city.
3 Bill flies to Madrid every week.
4 I sometimes take a taxi home from the station.
5 Jane often falls when she rides her bike.
6 Paul often misses the 7.30 bus to school.
7 The taxi driver usually helps the old lady to carry her luggage to the train.
8 Susie usually dances very well.

47.5 Answer these questions. Use *every day, once a week, once a year* or *never*.

1 How often do you walk to work or school?   I walk to work every day.
2 Have you got a bike? How often do you ride it?
3 How often do you go swimming? Do you swim in the sea or in a pool?
4 How often do you go somewhere by plane?
5 How often do you drive a car?
6 How often do you go dancing?
7 Do you often go climbing?
8 How often do you take a taxi?

Language words

This book uses some grammar words in English.

grammar word	meaning	example	in your language
noun	a person or thing	book, girl, pen	
pronoun	used instead of a noun	I, he, she, we, it, mine, yours	
verb	something we do	do, read, write	
adjective	describes a person or thing	good, bad, happy, long	
adverb	describes a verb	slowly, badly	
preposition	a little word used before a noun or pronoun	in, on, by, at	
conjunction	connects one part of a sentence to another	and, because, if, so, after, when	
singular	just one	book, house	
plural	more than one	books, houses	
phrase	a group of words (not a complete sentence)	in a house, at home, an old man	
sentence	a complete idea in writing, beginning with a capital letter and ending with a full stop	The man went into the room and closed the door.	
paragraph	a short part of a text (one or more sentences) beginning on a new line	This book has 60 units. Each unit has two pages.	
dialogue	a conversation between two people	Ann: How's Jo? Bill: OK, thanks.	
question	a set of words that begin with a capital letter and end with a question mark	Are you English? Do you like school?	
answer	a reply to a question	Yes, I am. No, I don't.	

Tip

When you learn a new word, make a note of the type of word it is in your notebook.
e.g. happy – adjective, in – preposition

Exercises

48.1 Write the grammar words opposite in your own language.

48.2 Write these words in the correct column.

~~book~~ speak good word house have write new man right blue say

noun	verb	adjective
book		

48.3 Add three more examples of prepositions.

in,..

48.4 Are the following phrases, sentences or questions?

1 in the park   phrase
2 Do you speak English?
3 a black cat
4 She's writing a book.
5 What's your name?
6 I like English.

48.5 Answer these questions.

1 What is the plural of **book**?   books
2 What is the singular of **men**?
3 Is **from** a verb?
4 Is **cat** an adjective?
5 Is this a phrase? '**Jane loves Harry.**'
6 Is **bad** an adverb?
7 What type of word are **we** and **it**?
8 Which of these words is a conjunction: **good, us, because**?

48.6 In this text, find four nouns, one adjective, one adverb, one preposition, and one pronoun.

The cat plays happily in the garden all day. She loves fresh milk.

Nouns: .cat,..

Adjective: ....

Adverb: ....

Preposition: ....

Pronoun: ....

49 Conjunctions and connecting words

A
A Basic conjunctions

Conjunctions join two parts of a sentence. They help to show the connection between the two parts of the sentence.

conjunction	example	use
and	Kate is a student **and** she works part-time.	We use *and* to give extra information in the second part of the sentence.
but	They are rich **but** they aren't happy.	We use *but* when the second part of the sentence contrasts with the first part.
or	You can pay by credit card **or** cash.	We use *or* when the second part of the sentence gives a different possibility.
because	We went home early **because** we were tired.	We use *because* when the second part of the sentence explains why the first part happened.
so	I felt ill **so** I didn't go to work.	We use *so* when the second part of the sentence gives a result of the first part.
when	I went to the party **when** the babysitter arrived.	We use *when* to say when the first part of the sentence happened.
before	We left **before** it started to rain.	We use *before* to show that the first part of the sentence happened first.
after	We went for a meal **after** we had seen the film.	We use *after* to show that the second part of the sentence happened first.
if	You can have some ice cream **if** you eat your dinner.	We use *if* to say that the first part of the sentence will only happen after the second part of the sentence happens and it may not happen.

B Other connecting words

These words are useful for making connections between words and phrases.

word	example	use
only	He **only** sleeps for three hours every night.	We use *only* to say something is not very big or very much.
like	She looks **like** her father.	We use *like* to make a comparison.
than	She works harder **than** he does.	We use *than* after a comparative adjective or adverb.
also too as well	He works in the shop and she does **also / too / as well**.	We use *also*, *too* and *as well* to say something is extra.

> **Tip**
>
> These words are small, but they are very important to learn. Write a translation of the words in the first column of the tables.

Exercises

49.1 Choose one of the words to complete each sentence.

1 Sam liked school (because) / but / if he had many friends there.
2 Sam left school so / or / and he joined the navy.
3 He hadn't travelled much but / before / after he joined the navy.
4 Sam was seasick when / if / so he left the navy.
5 He took a job in a bank because / after / or it was near his home.
6 He will stay at the bank when / if / before he likes it there.
7 If he doesn't like his new job, he'll go to university before / if / or he'll move to London.
8 He wants to get married if / when / so he's 25.

49.2 Write down nine sentences from the columns. Use each of the conjunctions once.

Mary agreed to marry Sanjay after they decided to set up a business together.

Mary agreed to marry Sanjay	after	she loves him.
	and	she loved him.
	because	she doesn't love him.
	before	they had two sons.
	but	he moves to London.
	if	he moved to London.
	or	she won't marry anyone.
Mary will marry Sanjay	so	he was a pop star.
	when	they decided to set up a business together.

49.3 Fill in the gaps with words from B opposite.

I love swimming, my brother loves swimming ¹ too and my sister likes it very much ² .... I can swim better ³ .... they can! Almost all my family loves swimming. My grandmother swims ⁴ .... a fish but she doesn't swim very often – ⁵ .... every year or so, now.

49.4 Write six sentences about your family and your habits using *only, than, like, also, too* and *as well*.

I play tennis and my mother plays as well. My mother plays better than I do.

49.5 Complete these sentences about yourself.

1 I'm learning English because ....
2 I'll learn more English if ....
3 I'm learning English and ....
4 I started learning English when ....
5 I can speak some English, so ....
6 I'll learn more English but ....

50 Days, months, seasons

A Time

There are:
365 **days** in a **year** (a year which has 366 days is a **leap year**)
12 **months** /mʌnθs/ in a year
7 days in a **week**
2 weeks in a **fortnight**
24 **hours** in a day
60 **minutes** in an hour (we say **an hour** /'aʊə/)
60 **seconds** in a minute
100 years in a **century**

B Days of the week

Sunday /'sʌndeɪ/, **Monday** /'mʌndeɪ/, Tuesday, Wednesday /'wenzdeɪ/, Thursday, Friday, Saturday

The names of the days always begin with a capital letter in English.

Saturday + Sunday = **the weekend**

| the day before yesterday | ← yesterday ← | today | → tomorrow → | the day after tomorrow |

Monday (before 12 am) = Monday **morning**

Monday (between 12 am and 6 pm) = Monday **afternoon**

Monday (after 6 pm) = Monday **evening**

We say **on** + days of the week: on Monday, on Saturday, etc. I saw her **on Friday** / **on Tuesday** evening.

> **Error warning**
> We say **at** + the weekend: I went to the cinema **at** the weekend [NOT ~~in the~~ weekend].

C Months and seasons

Months: January, February, March, April, May, June, July, August, September, October, November, December

The names of the months always begin with a capital letter in English.

Some countries have four **seasons: spring, summer, autumn** /'ɔːtəm/ and **winter**.

The names of the seasons do not usually begin with a capital letter in English.

We say **in** + months / seasons: **in July, in December, in (the) spring, in (the) summer,** etc.

Birds sing **in (the) spring**.

> **Error warning**
> My birthday is **in** July [NOT ~~on~~ July].

> **Tip**
> Write the day and date in English every time you do an English exercise, e.g. **Thursday 9th December 2010**.

Exercises

50.1   **Answer these questions.**

1 24 hours = *one day*
2 100 years = ...
3 2 weeks = ...
4 60 minutes = ...
5 7 days = ...

50.2   **Complete this British children's song about the number of days in each month.**

Thirty days has S*eptember* .... ,

A........................ , J........................ and N........................... .

All the rest have .... ,

Except for F............................ ,

Which has twenty-eight days

And .... in each leap year.

50.3   **These abbreviations are often used for the days of the week and the months. Write the names out in full.**

1 Mon *Monday*
2 Aug ....
3 Oct ....
4 Sat ....

5 Wed ....
6 Jan ....
7 Apr ....
8 Fri ....

9 Feb ....
10 Sept ....
11 Tues ....
12 Nov ....

50.4   **What are the next letters in each of these? Why?**

1 S S *A W* (the first letters of the four seasons: spring, summer, autumn, winter)
2 S M T W ....
3 J F M A M J J ....

50.5   **Correct the six mistakes in this paragraph.**

                                   S
I'm going to a party on Saturday for Jill's birthday. Her birthday is on thursday but she wanted to have the party in the weekend. She's having a barbecue. I think june is a good month to have a birthday because of the weather. I love going to barbecues on the summer. My birthday is in Winter and it's too cold to eat outside!

50.6   **How quickly can you answer these quiz questions?**

1 How many minutes are there in a quarter of an hour?
2 What is the third day of the week?
3 How many seconds are there in five minutes?
4 What is the seventh month?
5 How many months are there in ten years?
6 What month is your birthday in?
7 What day is it today?
8 What day will it be tomorrow?
9 What day will it be the day after tomorrow?
10 What day was it yesterday?
11 What day was it the day before yesterday?
12 What month is it?

51 Time words

A Time in relation to now

Now means at this moment. **Then** means at another moment (usually in the past).

I was born in Edinburgh. **Then** we moved to London. **Now** I live in Cambridge.

It is 10 **o'clock** now.

I got up **four hours ago, at** 6 o'clock.

An hour ago it was 9 o'clock.

two years	**for two years**
2008–2010	from 2008 to 2010

2008 ⟶ 2010

last year / last week / last Saturday

next year / next week / next summer

It is July **now**.

Last month it was June.

Next month it will be August.

When we talk about time in general, we talk about **the past, the present** and **the future**.

In the past people didn't have television.

People may travel to Mars **in the future**.

B Frequency adverbs

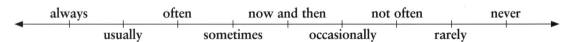

It **always** snows in Russia in winter.

It **often** rains in the UK.

The Ancient Romans **never** went to America or Australia.

C Expressions

Notice the use of **a** in these expressions of frequency.

once [one time] **a week**: I go swimming **once a week**, every Saturday.

twice [two times] **a day**: I clean my teeth **twice a day**.

three times a year: I see my uncle **three times a year**.

four times a month: I play football **four or five times a month**.

I'll be with you **in a moment**. [a very short time]

Jane's in Paris **at the moment**. [now]

See you **soon**! [in a short time]

We met **recently**. [not long ago]

Exercises

51.1 Fill the gaps with a preposition from the opposite page.

¹In............... the past, Rosa worked in many different countries. Rosa worked in Hong Kong ²............... three years, ³............... 1993 ⁴............... 1996. ⁵............... the moment she is working in Tokyo. She will stay there ⁶............... two more years.

51.2 Draw lines to match the centuries to their time.

1 the 19th century
2 the 22nd century   the past
3 the 18th century   the present
4 the 21st century   the future
5 the 20th century

51.3 Are these sentences true about you? If not, write them out correctly. Use other frequency adverbs from B opposite.

1 I always go swimming on Fridays.   *I sometimes go swimming on Fridays.*
2 I usually go to school / work by bus.
3 I occasionally watch TV.
4 I rarely drink milk.
5 I often wear a hat.
6 I rarely eat chocolate.
7 I always go to bed at 10.
8 I never go to the theatre.

51.4 Read the sentences and answer the questions.

1 Peter will get his exam results very soon.
Do you think Peter will get them next year, next month or tomorrow?   *Probably tomorrow*
2 Harriet and Rupert met for the first time recently.
Do you think they first met last year, six months ago or a week ago?
3 I'll help you in a moment.
Do you think I'll help you next week, in two hours or in a few minutes?
4 It's 6 o'clock now.
Two hours ago it started to snow. What time was it then?

51.5 Look at the table and write sentences using expressions like *once a week, three times a month*, etc.

John plays tennis twice a week.

	play tennis	practise the piano	have a business meeting in Germany
John	Mondays and Thursdays	Saturdays	the first Friday every month
Bettina and Amy	Tuesdays, Fridays and Saturdays	every morning and every evening	once in January, March, May, July, August and December every year

52 Places

A General place words

Come **here**, please. [to me, to where I am]

Have you been to Lima? I'm going **there** in April. [not here, another place]

Jim is coming **back** from Portugal in May. [to here again, to this place]

There are books and papers **everywhere** in my room. [in all parts / all places]

(See **Unit 40: Come / came / come.**)

B Prepositions

Luke is **in the kitchen**, making dinner.

There are two restaurants **in the village**.

Martha lives **in Seoul / South Korea / Asia.**

in

I'll meet you **at the station.**

I always sit **at the front of the class.**

● at

I like that photo **on the wall.**

Don't put your books **on the chair.** I want to sit **on it!**

on

C Positions

the **top** of the mountain   the **middle** of the road   the **bottom** of the glass

the **front** of the car   the **side** of the car   the **back** of the car

the **beginning** of the motorway

the **end** of the motorway

D Left and right

This is his **left** hand. This is his **right** hand.

In York Street, there is a cinema **on the left** and a restaurant **on the right.**

left   right

E Home and away

Is Mary **at home**? [in her house / flat]

No, sorry, she's **out.** [not here for a short time, e.g. at the shops or at work]

No, sorry, she's **away.** [not here for a longer time, e.g. on holiday]

No, sorry, she's **abroad.** [in another country]

Exercises

52.1 Fill the gaps with *here, there, back* or *everywhere*.

1 Thanks for lending me your dictionary. I'll bring it .back........... soon. (See **Unit 42: Bring / brought / brought.**)
2 Come .... Emma! Don't go near the road! (See **Unit 40: Come / came / come.**)
3 This letter is for a teacher at the university. Can you take it .... (See **Unit 41: Take / took / taken.**)
4 I opened the washing machine too soon. Now there's water .... !
5 I want to leave this letter in Nora's office. Are you going .... ?
6 I'm going to Italy tomorrow, but I'm coming .... on Friday.

52.2 Fill the gaps with the correct preposition.

1 My brother works .in........... Paris.
2 Why do you always sit .... the back of the class?
3 Let's go and sit .... the sofa.
4 What time do you arrive? I'll meet you .... the bus station.
5 There was a picture of an old man .... the wall.
6 Do you usually study .... your bedroom or .... the living room?

52.3 Mark the positions on the bus and on the tree.

1 the front of the bus
2 the side of the bus
3 the back of the bus
4 the middle of the tree
5 the top of the tree
6 the bottom of the tree

the front of the bus

52.4 Fill the gaps with *out, away* or *abroad*.

1 I'd like to work .abroad............. and learn about a new country.
2 Is Lily here? No, she's .... but she'll be back in about five minutes.
3 I'm going .... tomorrow. I'm going to stay with my sister for a few days.
4 When we go .... we like to go .... and see new countries.

52.5 Answer these questions about yourself and about this book.

1 Are you studying English at home or abroad?
2 Are you going away this year?
3 What have you got in your left or right hand at the moment?
4 What is there at the end of this book?
5 Where is Unit 3 in this book? (beginning / middle / end?)
6 Where is Unit 36 in this book? (beginning / middle / end?)

53 Manner

Adjectives and adverbs can describe **manner**, i.e. *how* we do something.

A Fast and slow

adjectives   This is a **fast** car.   This is a **slow** car.
adverbs   This car goes very **fast**.   This car goes very **slowly**.

B Loud /laud/ and quiet /'kwaɪət/

adjectives   The music is too **loud**.   It's very **quiet** here.
adverbs   The children sang **loudly**.   The teacher speaks very **quietly**.
                                              We can't hear him.

C Good and bad

adjectives   She's a **good** driver.   He's a **bad** driver.
adverbs   She drives **well**.   He drives **badly**.

D Right and wrong

This sentence is **right**.   I like coffee very much.   [✓]
This sentence is **wrong**.   I like very much coffee.   [✗]

E Expressions with way

He's speaking **in a friendly way**.   She's speaking **in an unfriendly way**.

You're doing that **the wrong way**.
Let me show you **the right way** to do it.

Exercises

53.1 Complete the sentences.

1 This train is **slow**. It goes very ..slowly............. .
2 He is a **bad** singer. He sings very ....
3 She is always **loud**. She speaks very ....
4 He's a **fast** swimmer. He swims very ....
5 This girl is **quiet**. She always speaks ....
6 He's a **good** English-speaker. He speaks English ....

53.2 Complete the sentences.

1 Please don't play your radio so ..loudly............. – I'm trying to study.
2 Let's take the .... train, not the fast one.
3 Katie is very .... at French but bad at German.
4 Why is Fiona behaving .... an unfriendly way?
5 I hope this is the .... answer.
6 It is better to do something well than to do it ....
7 The children are playing very .... – they know that grandma is asleep.
8 Did I do this exercise .... right way?

53.3 Are the definitions right or wrong? Use a dictionary.

word	definition	right (✓)	wrong (✗)
suddenly	very slowly		✗
sadly	in an unhappy way		
strangely	not in a normal way		
quickly	very slowly		
easily	with no difficulty		

53.4 Complete these sentences about yourself and your friends or family.

1 My ..sister plays tennis.................... well.
2 My .... badly.
3 I .... fast.
4 My .... slow.
5 My .... quiet.
6 I .... loudly.
7 My .... in a friendly way.
8 I .... the right way.

54 Common uncountable nouns

A What are countable and uncountable nouns?

apples   shoes   plates

COUNTABLE You can count them: four apples, two shoes.

sugar   money   luggage

UNCOUNTABLE You can't count it. [NOT three ~~luggages~~]

Can I have **three apples** and **some sugar**, please?

Are these **shoes** yours? **Is** this **luggage** yours?

B Everyday uncountable nouns

This **furniture** is modern.

The **traffic** is bad today.

I'll give you some **advice** about your future.

He can give some useful **information** about Bangkok.

There is some bad **news** today.

It's terrible **weather** today.

Accommodation here is expensive.

I need some fresh **air**.

Studying is hard **work**.

Air **travel** is faster than rail **travel**.

C Food

A lot of uncountable nouns are kinds of food and drink.

rice   spaghetti   butter   bread   milk   water   tea   coffee

Note: When we want to say how much we want, we say **two loaves** of bread, **three litres** of milk, **a kilo** of rice.

> **Tip**
>
> When you learn a new noun, write it down in a phrase which shows if it is countable or uncountable.

Exercises

54.1 Fill the gaps with an uncountable noun from the opposite page.

1 I'd like to buy a car but I haven't got enough ...money........... .
2 Cows give us .... and ....
3 If you don't know what to do, ask your parents for some ....
4 The .... at the seaside is very good for you.
5 Rob left school last month and is now looking for ....
6 There is always a lot of .... in central London.

54.2 Match the words on the left with the words on the right.

1 heavy   information
2 useful   travel
3 bad   water
4 modern   luggage
5 brown   news
6 cold   furniture
7 space   bread

54.3 Fill the gaps with the correct form of the verb *be*.

1 Accommodation in the city centre ..is.............. expensive.
2 Spaghetti with Italian tomato sauce .... very good.
3 The weather in Scotland .... best in the autumn.
4 The news .... better today than it .... yesterday.
5 Travel .... the most important thing in Sam's life.
6 Their furniture .... very old and very beautiful.

54.4 Correct the mistakes in these sentences.

1 The news ~~are~~ not very good today.   *is*
2 Where can I get some informations about your country?
3 Let me give you an advice.
4 Cook these spaghetti for ten minutes.
5 Can I have a bread, please?
6 We need to buy some new furnitures.
7 The east of the country usually has a better weather than the west.
8 I must find a new accommodation soon.

Follow-up

Use a dictionary to check if these words are countable or uncountable and make a note of them in your vocabulary notebook:
equipment
biscuit
homework
vehicle

55 Common adjectives 1: Good and bad things

A Good adjectives

a **good** restaurant

an **excellent** restaurant

good ———————————————————————————————— very good
nice   lovely   great   wonderful   excellent

A: That's a **nice** jacket.
B: Thank you.

It's a **great** film. We all loved it.

A: It's a **lovely** day today! /'lʌvli/
B: Yes, it is.

A: Do you want to go to London on Saturday?
B: That's an **excellent** idea! [very good]

a **wonderful** view
/'wʌndəfəl/

B Bad adjectives

bad weather

My hair is **awful!**

The weather this summer was **very bad**.

Other words that mean very bad are **dreadful, horrible, terrible**:

The food in that café was **horrible**. Nobody liked it.

What's that **dreadful** smell?

I had a **terrible** day at work today.

The traffic's **terrible** at 5 o'clock on Fridays.

C Expressions

A: The train arrives at 7 o'clock; dinner is at 8 o'clock.
B: **Excellent! / Great! / Wonderful! / Lovely! / Perfect!**

Note: We often say **not bad** when we are speaking.

A: I get $500 a week in my job.
B: That's **not bad!** (= good!)

We use these adjectives with **how**:

A: I have to get up at 5.30 tomorrow.
B: Oh, **how awful! / how horrible!**

A: I've got a great new job in New York!
B: **How nice! / How wonderful! / How lovely!**

> **Error warning**
> How awful! / How horrible!
> [NOT ~~How bad!~~]

Exercises

55.1 Complete the sentences.

1 My hair's _awful_ . I must go to the hairdresser's.
2 The weather's .... I don't want to go out.
3 The traffic is .... in the city centre. Take the train.
4 That's a(n) .... idea! Let's do it!
5 How .... ! Three exams on the same day!
6 What a .... house! The sea is only 100 metres away!
7 My timetable's not .... I'm free on Wednesdays and Fridays.
8 We have a .... view of the mountains from our hotel room.

55.2 What can you say? Someone says to you ...

1 Do you like my new skirt?   _Yes, it's lovely!_
2 I have to get up at 4.30 tomorrow morning.
3 Do you want to go out for dinner tonight?
4 (_in your town_) Excuse me. Is there a good restaurant in this town?
5 What do you think of your English lessons?
6 Is it OK if I come to your house at 6.30 tomorrow evening?

55.3 Match the words on the left with an expression from the right.

1 Blue sky, sun 25°   a Wonderful news
2 Five stars (*****)   b Awful weather
3 I don't want to walk. Let's take a taxi.   c Lovely weather
4 90 out of 100 in an exam   d A very good idea
5 (_in summer_) Grey sky, wind, rain, 4°   e An excellent hotel

55.4 Put these words into the good or bad column. Use a dictionary.

~~dreadful~~   brilliant   marvellous   nasty   fine

good	bad
	dreadful

55.5 Now think of two nouns to go with each of the adjectives in 55.4.
Use a dictionary to help you.

dreadful _weather / film_
brilliant ....
marvellous ....
nasty ....
fine ....

56 Common adjectives 2: People

A Saying positive / good things about people

Nice is the most common word used for people who we like / who are good.

Olga's very **nice**.

Richard's a **nice** man.

If we want to make **nice** stronger, we can use **wonderful**.

Ron is a **wonderful** teacher. All the students love him.

If someone is good to other people, we use **kind**.

She's very **kind**; she helps me with the children.

My teacher is a **lovely** man. (I like him very much)

My friend Neil is very **easy-going**. [relaxed, easy to be with]

Maureen's a **happy** person. (*opposite:* an **unhappy** person)

All my friends are more **intelligent** than me. [clever]

B Saying negative / bad things about people

Marcia is **not very nice**.

Horrible is a lot stronger than 'not very nice'.

Margaret is a **horrible** woman; nobody likes her.

My uncle is a **difficult** person. He is never happy.

That waiter is **stupid**. I asked for coffee and he has given me tea! (**stupid** is a very strong word)

I don't like **selfish** people. [people who think only of themselves]

C Children

We often say that children are **good** or **well-behaved**. If they are not, we say they are **naughty**.

Tim is very **good / well-behaved**, but his sister is very **naughty**.

D Prepositions

Jean was nice / kind / wonderful **to** me when I was in hospital.

You were horrible **to** me yesterday!

It was nice / kind **of** you to remember my birthday.

Exercises

56.1 Complete B's sentences.

1 A: Jessica's very nice.
   B: She's more than nice, she's ~~wonderful!~~
2 A: Was Paul nice to you?
   B: No, he was really .... !
3 A: Let me carry your bag.
   B: Thanks, that's ....
4 A: Is your little cousin well-behaved?
   B: No, he's ....
5 A: Katie only thinks about herself.
   B: I know. She's really ....

56.2 Complete the word puzzle. Use the letters given and words from the opposite page. (Note that 'selfish' is the only word that reads across; all the other words read down.)

	2			4		6	
	o			d		e	
1 s	e	3 l	f	i	s	7 h	
t				e	-	r	
u		e		g			
p	e						
i		u					
d	y			b			
	t						

56.3 Circle the words that describe you.

> **I am:** easy-going   sometimes difficult   kind to animals   sometimes stupid
> happy   intelligent   selfish   horrible to some people   nice to my friends

56.4 Fill in the correct prepositions.

1 The teacher is never horrible ~~to~~.......................... the students.
2 It is kind .... you to help me.
3 Barbara was wonderful .... me when I needed a friend.
4 It was nice .... her to ring me.

Follow-up

Think of some people you like and some people you don't like and write sentences about them using vocabulary from this unit.
e.g. I don't like (name). He/She's horrible.

57 Words and prepositions

A Phrasal and prepositional verbs

Some verbs are used with different particles and prepositions.

I **listen to** the radio in bed in the morning.

I **waited for** the bus for half an hour yesterday.

I **asked for** a black coffee, not a white one.

Where do I **pay for** our meal?

I hope you can **come to** my party.

This book **belongs to** Sarah Smith.

What are you **thinking about**?

Helena **thanked** her mother **for** the present.

Jamie **apologised for** being late.

B Phrasal verbs

Some verbs have different meanings when they are used with different prepositions, for example, **look**.

I love **looking at** old photographs.

If you want to find your key, you must **look for** it.

Parents **look after** their children. [they take care of them]

You **look forward to** something nice in the future, for example, a friend's visit, or a holiday.

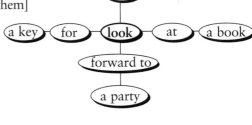

C Adjectives

Some adjectives are also followed by prepositions.

I'm **good at** geography but **bad at** maths.

I'm **interested in** (hearing) all your news.

He is **afraid of** mice.

Lucy is **proud of** winning a medal and her mother is proud of her.

Note: You are **used to** what you know well: I'm **used to** getting up early, I always do.

You have **to get used to** something new, for example a new school or driving on the other side of the road.

> ### Error warning
> She's a lovely person and I'm really happy about her success [NOT ~~happy for~~ her success].

D Grammar

Prepositions are followed by a noun: Joe is **good at tennis** or by the *-ing* form of the verb: Joe is **good at playing** the piano.

> ### Tip
> Look carefully at prepositions when you read in English. Make a note of any phrases which use prepositions in a new way.

Exercises

57.1 Match the words on the left with the words on the right.

1 John is waiting   a   for his mistake.
2 This bicycle belongs   b   about the holidays.
3 The children thanked their aunt   c   for a train to London.
4 Sally is listening   d   to the hotel.
5 He apologised   e   for our tickets.
6 Let me pay   f   to the football match.
7 Hamid is thinking   g   to her MP3 player.
8 Over 100 people came   h   for the money.

57.2 Complete these sentences using the appropriate preposition(s) and a word or phrase from the box.

~~books~~   the children   me   people   my party   it   a new one   them

1 Isabel's granddaughter can't read yet but she likes looking _at books_ .
2 A nurse looks ....
3 I can't find my glasses? Could you help me look .... ?
4 It's my birthday soon. I'm really looking ....
5 Why are you looking .... in that way? Is my face dirty?
6 I don't like my job very much. I'm looking ....
7 Alex is going to France in July. He is looking ....
8 I often look .... when their parents go out.

57.3 Write prepositions.

Anne has got used [1] _to_ .... her new school and is doing well there. She is very good [2] .... English and maths. She always listens [3] .... her teachers. She is very interested [4] .... sport and she belongs [5] .... a tennis club and a swimming club. Her parents were very proud [6] .... her when she won a medal for swimming last month. Anne was very happy [7] .... her medal too, of course. She showed it to me when she came [8] .... my house last Saturday.

57.4 Hiroshi is a visitor from Japan. Make sentences about what he found strange (✗) in Britain and what he didn't find strange (✓).

1 speaking English every day ✗   He wasn't used to speaking English every day.
2 driving on the left ✓   Hiroshi was used to driving on the left.
3 eating British food ✗
4 traffic jams ✓
5 expensive shops ✓
6 British money ✗

57.5 Answer the questions about yourself.

1 What are / were you good at at school? What are / were you bad at?
2 What do you usually ask for when you go to a café?
3 What are you proud of?
4 What are you afraid of?
5 What kind of music do you like listening to?
6 What are you looking forward to?
7 Do you belong to any clubs?
8 Are you used to eating different kinds of food?

58 Prefixes

Prefixes (at the beginning of words) can help you to understand what a new word means. Here are some common prefixes.

prefix	meaning	examples
ex (+ noun)	was but now isn't	**ex-wife, ex-president**
half (+ noun or adjective)	50% of something	**half-price, half-hour**
in, im (+ adjective)	not	**informal, impossible**
non (+ adjective or noun)	not	**non-smoking**
pre (+ noun, adjective, verb)	before	**pre-school, pre-heat**
re (+ verb)	again	**redo, rewrite**
un (+ adjective or noun)	not	**unhappy, unsafe**

An **ex-wife** is a wife who is now divorced.

President Bush is an **ex-president** of the USA.

Something that cost £10 yesterday and costs £5 today is **half-price**.

A **half-hour** journey is a journey of 30 minutes.

Informal clothes are clothes like jeans and trainers. Formal clothes are things like a suit.

If something is **impossible**, you can't do it. It's impossible to read with your eyes closed.

You must not smoke in a **non-smoking** restaurant.

Pre-school children are too young to go to school.

You nearly always need to **pre-heat** the oven before you cook something.

To **redo** something is to do it a second time, and to **rewrite** something is to write it a second time.

Unhappy means sad, the opposite of happy.

Unsafe means dangerous, the opposite of safe.

THIS BRIDGE IS UNSAFE!

Tip

Sometimes words with prefixes have a hyphen (-), e.g. a half-hour programme, and sometimes they don't, e.g. an impossible question. Use a dictionary when you are not sure if there is a hyphen or not.

Exercises

58.1 Choose one of the words from the opposite page to fit in these sentences.

1 This part of the restaurant is _non-smoking_.
2 I can't read this. Please .... your homework.
3 In .... English we often say 'Hi', not 'Good morning'.
4 I liked school but my sister was very .... there.
5 I bought two T-shirts because they were .... in the sale.
6 Don't walk on that wall – the notice says it is ....

58.2 Write your own sentences to show what these words mean.

1 ex-wife   _Jennifer Aniston is Brad Pitt's ex-wife._
2 ex-president   ....
3 redo   ....
4 impossible   ....
5 pre-school   ....

58.3 What do you think these words and phrases mean? Look at the table opposite to help you.

1 an ex-husband   _a husband who is now divorced from his wife_
2 pre-exam nerves
3 an incorrect answer
4 an unread book
5 to retell a story
6 a half-brother
7 an unfinished letter
8 a non-alcoholic drink
9 to reread a book
10 to resend an email

58.4 Find the negative forms of these words. Use a dictionary to help you.

1 possible   _impossible_
2 comfortable
3 polite
4 pleasant
5 attractive

Follow-up

Look at the table opposite and write one more example of a word using each prefix. Use a dictionary to help you. Write a sentence using your word.

ex: My ex-boss lives near me.

half: You stop at half-time in a football match.

Suffixes come at the end of words. They help you to understand the meaning of a new word. Here are some common suffixes.

suffix	meaning	examples
er, or (noun)	person	**worker, swimmer, instructor**
er, or (noun)	machine, thing	**cooker, calculator**
ful (adjective)	full of	**useful, beautiful**
less (adjective)	without	**useless, endless**
ly	makes an adverb from an adjective	**quickly, happily**
ness	makes an abstract noun from an adjective	**happiness, sadness**
y	makes an adjective from a noun	**sandy, sunny**

He's a hard **worker**. He works 12 hours a day.

She's a very good **swimmer**. She was in the Olympic team.

Her tennis is much better now that she has a new **instructor**.

We've got a new gas **cooker** so the food should be delicious!

Can we use our **calculators** in the maths test?

Thanks for the information. It was very **useful**.

What a **beautiful** photo. I think it will win the competition.

This book is no help at all – it's **useless**.

I can't finish this book – it's **endless**.

He was late for work so he went **quickly** to the station.

They are **happily** married with two young children.

The mother was smiling with **happiness** as she held her baby in her arms.

They said goodbye with great **sadness** because they knew they would probably never meet again.

That beach is very popular with tourists because it is long and **sandy**.

It's a lovely **sunny** day – let's go to the beach.

Exercises

59.1 Which of the example words from the opposite page do these pictures illustrate?

1 a s.unny. day.........................

3 a s..

5 a c...

2 a golf i.................................

4 He's smiling h.........................

6 a u.................................... thing

59.2 Find the adjectives and match them with the nouns they go with in the box. Some adjectives can go with more than one noun.

| ~~electric~~ worker fast beautiful cooker sandy weather sunny car hard idea |
| useful book endless swimmer beach guitar smile picture fun useless |

1 _electric cooker / guitar_ ....
2 ....
3 ....
4 ....
5 ....

6 ....
7 ....
8 ....
9 ....

59.3 Complete the sentences using the word in brackets and a suffix.

1 Can I use your bottle _opener_............... , please? (open)
2 I'm tired because I slept very .... last night. (bad)
3 The waiter was very .... and explained everything on the menu. (help)
4 Thank you very much for all your .... (kind)
5 It's important not to make .... mistakes in your writing. (care)
6 It was wet and .... most of last week. (wind)
7 I did the homework very .... (easy)
8 Do you know a good .... who could do some work on our house? (build)

59.4 What do you think these words and phrases mean? Use the information about suffixes from the opposite page to help you.

1 a hair dryer   _a thing that you use to dry your hair_
2 a traveller
3 slowly
4 hopeful
5 rainy
6 painless
7 badly
8 a tin opener
9 a footballer
10 snowy

60 Words you may confuse

This unit looks at words which are easy to mix up.

A Similar sounds

quite /kwaɪt/ / **quiet** /ˈkwaɪət/

This book is **quite** good. ──▶ bad ──▶ quite good ──▶ good

My bedroom is very **quiet**. (= silent)

lose /luːz/ / **loose** /luːs/

A: Why do I always **lose** my keys!
B: Here they are.
A: Oh, thank you!

If you **lose** something, you do not know where it is / you can't find it.

These trousers are very **loose**. (loose means they are not tight, because they are too big)

fell / felt

Fell is the past of **fall**.

Yesterday I **fell** and broke my arm.

Felt is the past of **feel**.

I **felt** ill yesterday, but I **feel** OK today.

cook / cooker

He is a very good **cook**. [the person who cooks]

This **cooker** costs £500. [the thing you cook on]

B Similar or related meanings

lend / borrow

If you **lend** something, you *give* it.

If you **borrow** something, you *get* it.

Sam wants a bicycle:

> Do you want to borrow it?

SAM: Will you **lend** me your bicycle? (= you *give* it to me for one day / an hour, etc.)

or Can I **borrow** your bicycle? (= I *get* it from you)

RITA: Yes, take it.

SAM: Thanks.

check / control

The passport officer **checked** my passport. [looked at it]

We use the mouse to **control** the computer. [tell it what to do]

C Other words often mixed up

They're **waiting for** the bus.

I **hope** I pass my exams. [I really want to pass]

I haven't studied; I **expect** I'll fail my exams. [it's probable]

In English the **afternoon** is from about 12 o'clock till 5 or 6 pm.

The **evening** is from 5 or 6 pm until about 9 or 10 pm.

After 9 or 10 pm it is the **night**.

Exercises

60.1 Fill the gaps with words from A opposite. The first letter is given.

1 Please be q̲u̲i̲e̲t̲ . The baby is sleeping.
2 If you l.................... your passport you must call the embassy.
3 I f.................... tired this morning, but I am OK now.
4 We are going to buy a c.................... for our new kitchen.
5 She f.................... and broke her leg. She had to go to hospital.
6 It's q.................... cold today.
7 Do you have this skirt in a smaller size? This one is too l.................... .
8 My sister is a good c.................... . I love eating at her house.

60.2 What does each word below sound like? Circle the correct word.

1 lose   *juice*   (*shoes*)
2 loose   *juice*   *shoes*
3 quite   *right*   *higher*
4 quiet   *right*   *higher*

60.3 Answer these questions.

1 Why do we use a mouse with a computer? To c̲o̲n̲t̲r̲o̲l̲ ̲i̲t̲.
2 What does the passport officer do to your passport? He/She ....
3 If you want to use someone's camera for two hours, what do you say?
  Can I .... ?
4 What do you say to someone at 3 pm? Good ....
5 What do people do at a bus stop? They ....
6 What do you say to a friend if you need £1?
  Can you .... ?
7 What do you say if someone makes too much noise? Please be ....

60.4 Answer these questions.

1 Are you expecting any visitors today?
2 What do you hope to do this summer?
3 Do you borrow things from your friends? What things?
4 Would you lend £100 to your best friend?

Look at these units to find other words that are often confused:

Do and **make**	**Units 38 and 39**
Take and **bring**	**Units 41 and 42**
Say, tell, speak and **talk**	**Unit 46**
Rob and **steal**	**Unit 32**

Follow-up

Look up these pairs of verbs in a dictionary and make notes on the difference in meaning:

1 lie – lay – lain
  lay – laid – laid

2 rise – rose – risen
  raise – raised – raised

Answer key

Unit 1

1.1
2 brother
3 aunt
4 uncle
5 grandmother
6 grandfather
7 nephew
8 niece
9 mother
10 wife
11 cousin

1.2
2 aunt
3 only child
4 father
5 wife
6 mother
7 grandchildren
8 wives
9 grandparents (parents is also a possible answer)

1.3 *Possible answers:*

1 Chen has / has got one brother and one sister.
2 Chen has / has got two cousins.
3 Chen has / has got two nephews but he hasn't got any nieces.
4 Chen has / has got only one grandmother now.
5 Chen doesn't come from a very big family.

1.4 *Your own answer*

Follow-up

Possible family tree:

I am José. Ana Maria is my wife. Javier and Isabella are our children. Javier is our son and Isabella is our daughter. Rosa is our niece. Antonio, Pedro and Juan are our nephews. Carla and Luis are my parents. Jorge is my brother and Dolores and Consuela are my sisters.

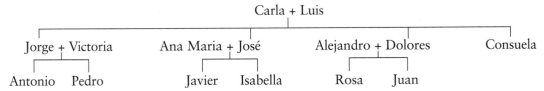

Unit 2

2.1 *Possible answers:*

2 My father was born in South Africa on June 4th 1949.
3 My brother was born in London on June 6th 1974.
4 My husband was born in Russia on February 6th 1969.
5 My son was born in Cambridge on October 16th 1995.

2.2
2 (bride)groom
3 single
4 weigh
5 divorced
6 funeral
7 honeymoon
8 widowed

2.3 2 to 3 of 4 on 5 born 6 after

2.4 2 Christopher Columbus was born in 1451 and died in 1506.
3 Leonardo da Vinci was born in 1452 and died in 1519.
4 Princess Diana was born in 1961 and died in 1997.
5 Heath Ledger was born in 1979 and died in 2008.

2.5 2 death 3 dead 4 died 5 dead

2.6 *Possible answer:*

I have one brother and one sister. My sister got married this year. For her honeymoon, she went to Italy. My brother has two children. They were born in 2001 and 2008.

Unit 3

3.1
2 nose		7 tooth	
3 heart		8 thumb	
4 stomach		9 back	
5 shoulder		10 waist	
6 ear			

3.2
2 toes		6 ears
3 teeth		7 knee / shoulders
4 nose		8 blood
5 heart		9 brain

3.3 2 That woman has got very big **feet**.
3 My grandfather has a pain in **his** shoulder.
4 The baby has already got two **teeth**.
5 The little girl needs to wash **her** face and **her** hands before dinner.
6 My **hair is** dirty. I need to wash **it**.

3.4
2 football	5 headscarf
3 lipstick	6 handbag
4 hairbrush	

Follow-up

1 b arms c legs
2 The eye is the hole in the needle.
3 The face is the front of the clock (with the numbers on it). The big hand shows the minutes and the little hand shows the hours.
4 The neck is the narrow part at the top of the bottle.
5 The foot of the mountain is the bottom of the mountain (the lowest part).

Unit 4

4.1 1 suit, shirt, tie
2 T-shirt, shorts
3 socks, trainers
4 carrying, bag
5 belt
6 jacket, coat

4.2
2 belt – waist
3 hat – head
4 glasses – eyes
5 shoe – foot
6 glove – hand
7 tights – legs
8 scarf – neck

4.3
1 is
2 is wearing
3 has; is carrying
4 is; are
5 were; are
6 Is
7 are
8 is wearing / has

4.4
2 jumper
3 watch
4 skirt
5 bag
6 hat
7 shirt
8 coat
9 umbrella
10 boots

4.5

morning	night
get dressed	get undressed
or put your clothes on	*or* take your clothes off

4.6 *Possible answer:*

I'm wearing a blue T-shirt and black trousers. I've got white shoes on. I'm wearing a watch, three rings and a pair of glasses.

Unit 5

5.1
2 tall
3 slim / thin
4 fair
5 young
6 fat / overweight
7 elderly

5.2
2 Is Elena's hair blonde / fair?
3 Is Mike's hair long?
4 Are your parents elderly? (Are your parents old? is a less polite question)
5 Is his sister pretty / beautiful?
6 Why is Sara so thin?

5.3 *Possible answers:*

2 Jeff has short fair hair and a beard.
3 Caroline's got dark skin and dark hair.
4 Stefan's hair is long and he has a moustache.

5.4
2 What does your teacher look like?
3 How much do you weigh? / How heavy are you?
4 How old is your mother?
5 How tall is your sister?
6 What do your parents look like?

5.5 *Possible answers:*

2 She's tall and slim with blonde hair.
3 I'm 75 kilos. I'm not overweight but I'm not thin.
4 She's middle-aged. She's 49.
5 She's very tall for her age. She's 1 metre 58.
6 They're medium height. My mother has long dark hair and my father has fair hair and a beard and a moustache.

Follow-up

Possible answers:

Joanna: Joanna is tall. She has long black hair and brown eyes. She's very pretty.
Kevin: Kevin is medium height. He has fair hair and a beard. His eyes are blue. He's average-looking.
My mother: My mother is short with grey hair. She has green eyes. She's beautiful.

Unit 6

6.1 **2** I feel sick. / I don't feel very well. / I feel ill.
3 feel ill.
4 I've got toothache.
5 a cold

6.2

illness	treatment
a headache	take an aspirin
toothache	go to the dentist
a heart attack	go to hospital
a cold	go to bed with a hot drink

6.3 **2** cholera   **4** hay fever
3 asthma   **5** cancer / heart attacks

6.4 *Possible answers:*

1 Yes, I eat a lot of fruit and vegetables, and not many sweet things.
2 I like / love swimming and cycling.
3 Yes, I feel stressed when I have exams.
4 Yes, I had an operation once / I broke my leg, etc. ('Be in hospital' means you are ill, you are a patient. 'Be in a hospital' can just mean you are visiting someone.)

Unit 7

7.1 *Possible answers:*

2 I hate cowboy films.   6 I love cats.
3 I like flying.   7 I like cars.
4 I like tea.   8 I don't like jazz music.
5 I don't like football.

7.2 *Possible answers:*

2 I prefer cats to dogs.
3 I prefer sightseeing to sunbathing.
4 I prefer cars to bikes.
5 I prefer strawberry to chocolate ice cream.
6 I prefer watching sport to doing sport.

7.3 *Possible answers:*

2 I hope (that) the lesson ends soon.
3 I want some food.
4 I hope (that) my friend feels better soon.
5 I want to go to bed.
6 I want to cry.
7 I hope (that) it gets hotter soon.
8 I want him/her to feel / be happy again soon.

7.4 2 Fred is thirsty.   5 Fiona is surprised.
3 William is cold.   6 The children are hot.
4 Sunita is tired.

7.5 2 I am happy **about** my sister's good news.
3 The teacher wants **us to** learn these new words.
4 I **really like** spiders.
5 My brother has a good new job. I'm very happy **for** him.
6 My parents want **me to** go to university.
7 I feel very well. How **about** you?
8 Priya is **a bit** tired this morning.

Follow-up

Possible answers:

2 I felt surprised yesterday when an old friend rang me.
3 I felt upset when my boss was rude to me.
4 I felt hungry when I saw some chocolate in a shop window.

Unit 8

8.1 2 Good luck!   6 Fine, thanks.
3 Congratulations! / Well done!   7 Hello! / Hi!
4 Goodbye.   8 Thank you.
5 Happy Birthday!

8.2 2 Happy Christmas!   5 Cheers!
3 Sorry!   6 Good morning!
4 Congratulations!

8.3 2 Thank you. Cheers!   6 Happy New Year!
3 Goodnight. Sleep well.   7 Sorry!
4 Good morning.   8 Happy Christmas!
5 Good afternoon.

8.4 *Possible answers:*

ANN: How are you?
YOU: Fine, thanks.
ANN: It's my birthday today.
YOU: Happy birthday!
ANN: Would you like a drink?
YOU: Yes, please. An orange juice.
ANN: Here you are. Cheers!
YOU: Cheers!

8.5 *Possible answer:*

A: Hello, good morning.
B: Hi. How are you?
A: Fine, thanks. And you?
B: Fine. A bit nervous. I'm taking my driving test today.
A: Good luck! That's funny, I passed mine last week.
B: Oh, congratulations!
A: It's my birthday today.
B: Is it? Happy Birthday! Why don't we go out for a drink this evening?
A: OK. See you later. Goodbye.
B: Goodbye. See you soon.

Unit 9

9.1 2 around 5 actually (really is also possible)
3 really 6 around
4 else

9.2 2 mind 3 Let's 4 Be careful 5 anyway

9.3 2 Look out! 5 Hurry up!
3 What a pity! 6 Well done!
4 It's up to you.

9.4 VERA: We need to celebrate. I got a new job!
LUKE: Well **done**! How about **going** out for a meal this evening?
VERA: Great! **Let's** go to that Italian restaurant. Or do you prefer the Chinese one?
LUKE: I don't **mind**. I like the Italian one but it's very expensive.
VERA: Oh, it **doesn't** matter.
LUKE: OK. Why don't we **go** to the Italian restaurant and then we could go to the cinema afterwards? Your new job needs a special celebration.
VERA: **I agree**. And I'd love to see that film with George Clooney. Would you?
LUKE: **Absolutely!**

Unit 10

10.1 2 Pasta; pizza (in either order) 5 meat
3 potatoes 6 hot dog
4 fish and chips

10.2

fruit	vegetables
pineapple	beans
grapes	onions
apple	carrot
pear	garlic
	mushrooms

10.3 2 strawberry 5 potatoes
3 peas 6 tomatoes
4 apple

10.4 2 beer 5 fruit juice
3 milk 6 mineral water
4 coffee

10.5 2 c 3 c 4 b 5 a 6 c

10.6 *Possible answer:*

My favourite foods are pizza, fish, strawberries and pineapple.
My favourite drinks are tea, coffee and fruit juice.
They are quite good for you.

Unit 11

11.1 2 yes
3 yes
4 no, the freezer is colder than the fridge
5 yes
6 no, a tea towel is for drying plates

11.2 *Possible questions*:

2 Where's the saucepan / frying pan?
3 Where do these bowls go?
4 Can I help with the washing-up?
5 Where can I find the milk?

11.3 *Possible answers*:

2 a cup, a teapot, a spoon
3 a frying pan, a cooker
4 a plate or bowl, a knife and fork, or a spoon and fork, or chopsticks
5 a glass or a cup or a mug
6 a microwave
7 washing-up liquid, a sink and a cloth or a dishwasher
8 a washing machine

11.4 2 a frying pan and a glass
3 a teapot and a tea towel (*or* cloth)
4 on the worktop next to the cooker
5 a kitchen roll
6 (a cupboard with) a bin and a cloth

Unit 12

12.1 2 wardrobe
3 chest of drawers
4 mirror
5 hairbrush
6 comb
7 bed
8 alarm clock
9 bedside lamp
10 bedside table

12.2 *Possible answers*:

toothpaste, hairbrush, comb, pyjamas, shower gel

12.3 2 Selim and Umit are washing their faces.
3 Mrs Park is going downstairs.
4 Mr Park is having a bath.
5 Jaime is getting dressed.
6 Lee is turning off the light.

12.4 *Possible answers*:

bath, shower, toilet, basin, soap, shower gel, shampoo, toothbrush, toothpaste, hairbrush, comb, razor, mirror, bathroom cupboard, shelf

12.5 *Possible answers*:

2 My bedroom has two windows.
3 In my bedroom there is a small bed.
4 There is one wardrobe on the right of the room.
5 True
6 I've got a lamp, some books, a radio and an alarm clock on my bedside table.
7 There is a chest of drawers next to the wardrobe.
8 I have got a dressing table.

12.6 2 10.30 (for example) 6 off   10 shower / bath
3 undressed   7 fall   11 clean
4 get   8 wake   12 get
5 for   9 up

Unit 13

13.1 2 a sofa   6 a hi-fi
3 a coffee table   7 a carpet or rug
4 a picture   8 a remote control
5 a light switch

13.2 2 relax in an   armchair
3 close the   curtains
4 pass the   remote control
5 listen to the   radio
6 watch   TV

13.3 2 I don't often listen **to** the radio.
3 We need some more **bookshelves** in this room.
4 I watched television all evening yesterday. (not 'at')
5 It's dark now. Please **close** the curtains.
6 Jim has some very nice **furniture** in his house.

13.4

F	T	A	L	W	X	A	R	O	C	F	Y	D
E	R	L	S	O	C	K	E	T	U	I	I	U
D	K	A	G	L	N	T	B	C	R	I	E	F
R	E	M	O	T	E	C	O	N	T	R	O	L
A	Y	P	F	C	H	A	I	R	A	P	J	I
D	E	C	H	K	I	R	G	T	I	R	U	G
I	B	O	O	K	F	P	S	I	N	E	B	H
O	G	F	E	A	I	E	L	H	S	C	R	T
S	U	A	T	L	E	T	V	C	A	E	U	O

Follow-up

Possible answer:

In my living room there is not much furniture. There is a table, a TV, a desk, a sofa and two armchairs. The walls are white and there are some pictures on them. I like to relax in the living room. In the evening I watch TV there, or listen to music.

Unit 14

14.1 2 A doctor works in a hospital (or a clinic, or a surgery).
3 A waiter works in a restaurant (or a café).
4 A secretary works in an office.
5 A shop assistant works in a shop.
6 A hairdresser works in a beauty salon (or a hairdresser's).

14.2 2 engineer
3 taxi driver
4 nurse
5 mechanic
6 secretary

14.3

Across	Down
1 bus driver	1 doctor
2 teacher	2 waiter
3 writer	3 nurse

14.4

2 engineer	5 clerk
3 warden	6 officer
4 librarian	

14.5 *Possible answers:*

1 I'm a teacher.   2 In a university.   3 Yes, very interesting.

Unit 15

15.1

2 d	4 f	6 i	8 a
3 g	5 b	7 e	9 h

15.2 ruler, pencil sharpener, board rubber, rubber, drawing pin, pencil, tape recorder, cassette, notepad, OHP

15.3 *Possible answer:*

In the room where I study English I can see a board, a noticeboard, a notebook, some pens, a pencil, a rubber and a pencil sharpener.

15.4

2 does	7 fails
3 passes	8 study
4 take / do	9 do
5 passes	10 get
6 go	

15.5 *Possible answer:*

My three favourite subjects were languages, English and art. I didn't like PE, physics and maths.

Unit 16

16.1 *Possible answer:*

I have the following: address, letter, envelope, stamp, phone number, phone, mobile, computer, screen, memory stick, mouse, keyboard, mobile device, CD-ROM, and email address.

16.2

2 phone box	6 address	10 laptop
3 mobile (phone)	7 envelope	11 memory stick
4 stamp	8 letter box	12 CD-ROM
5 mouse	9 screen	

16.3

2 speak	5 take (*or* give him)
3 sorry	6 call (*or* phone *or* ring)
4 at	

16.4 *Possible answers:*

1 01223 240754: oh one double two three, two four oh, seven five four
0207 4417895: oh two oh seven, double four one, seven eight nine five

2 steve@stuff.co.uk: Steve at stuff dot co dot U-K
katerina08@coldmail.com: katerina oh eight at coldmail dot com

16.5 *Possible answers:*

1 I prefer to phone my friends.   3 I go online several times a day.   5 I don't write letters
2 I send more emails.   4 I prefer to use a laptop.   very often.

Unit 17

17.1   2 going   3 time   4 by   5 send

17.2   2 a package holiday (or package tour)   4 a walking holiday
3 a coach tour   5 a winter holiday

17.3   *Possible answers:*

	you can take a lot of luggage	very fast	cheap	you see a lot as you travel	relaxing
ferry	✓✓		✓	✓✓	✓✓
car	✓✓✓	✓✓	✓✓	✓✓✓	✓
flight		✓✓✓	✓	✓	✓✓

17.4   2 passport   5 phrasebook
3 camera   6 tickets
4 luggage (or suitcase)

17.5   2 a visa   5 traveller's cheques
3 a plane   6 a suitcase
4 a rucksack

17.6   2 nightlife   3 local   4 postcard

Unit 18

18.1   2 toy shop   5 gift shop
3 butcher   6 baker
4 newsagent

18.2   2 a supermarket   5 a bookshop
3 the post office (or a newsagent)   6 a department store (or perhaps a supermarket)
4 a gift shop

18.3   2 ground floor   5 first floor   8 basement
3 fourth floor   6 second floor   9 third floor
4 basement   7 second floor   10 fourth floor

18.4   2 cash
3 (a £20) note
4 a credit card
5 change
6 a shop that sells meat
7 the floor above the ground floor (in a British building)
8 a shop that sells newspapers and magazines
9 the floor under the ground floor

18.5   2 Closed   3 Pull   4 Push   5 Open

18.6   1 cost   2 pay   3 (carrier) bag

Unit 19

19.1
2 shower   **5** hairdryer   **8** lift
3 TV   **6** sea
4 phone   **7** key

19.2   **2** a   **3** h   **4** f   **5** b   **6** g   **7** c   **8** e

19.3
1 At **reception** you can order **room** service.
2 We'd like a **double** room with a **view** of the garden, please.
3 The lift is **over** there. Take it to the second **floor**.
4 Please **fill** in this **form**.
5 I'd like a **wake-up call** at 7.30 and I'd like to **have** breakfast in my room, please.
6 I have a **reservation** for a **single** room with a bathroom.
7 Can I **have** the bill, please? I'll **check** it now.
8 I'm leaving today. Can I **exchange** some dollars here before I **check** out?

19.4   *Possible answers:*

Can I have breakfast in my room, please?
Can I have / check my bill, please?
Can I have a double room for tonight, please?
Can I have some help with my luggage? or Can I leave my luggage here, please?

19.5   *Possible answers:*

1 It costs about £100.
2 00 44 (from e.g. France)
3 Breakfast is usually from 7 to 10.
4 I think a TV is most important for me.

Unit 20

20.1   *Possible answers:*

2 restaurant   **4** café
3 fast food restaurant   **5** bar / pub

20.2   *Possible answers:*

2 café – Jim's Corner Café   **4** restaurant – The Taj Mahal
3 take-away – Corner Kebabs   **5** bar – The Red Lion

20.3   **2** curry   **3** salad   **4** pie   **5** steak

20.4
WAITER: Are you ready **to** order?
CUSTOMER: Yes, **I'd** like vegetable soup and steak, please.
WAITER: **How** would you like your steak? Rare, medium or **well-done**?
CUSTOMER: Rare, please.
WAITER: What **would you** like to drink?
CUSTOMER: **An** orange juice, please.

20.5   *Your own answers*

20.6   *Possible answers:*

1 I'd choose mixed salad, vegetable curry and ice cream.
2 Vegetarians can eat soup of the day, mixed salad and vegetable curry.
3 I like eating out very much.
4 I go to a restaurant two or three times a month.

Unit 21

21.1 **2** swimming **5** volleyball
3 judo / karate **6** motor racing
4 sailing

21.2 **2** badminton **6** basketball
3 table tennis **7** skiing
4 snowboarding **8** American football
5 baseball

21.3 **2** Do you play football?
3 Do you do any sports?
4 Do you go swimming? / like swimming? / swim?
5 What is your favourite sport?
6 Where do people play rugby?

21.4 *Possible answers:*

1 swimming, skiing, table tennis, tennis, kayaking
2 in a swimming pool, in the mountains, at home, at a sports centre, on a river
3 I like swimming, kayaking and table tennis.
4 I don't like tennis.
5 I'd like to go sailing.

Unit 22

22.1 **2** science fiction **6** romantic comedy
3 horror **7** thriller
4 action **8** musical
5 cartoon

22.2 *Possible answers:*

2 romantic comedy – *My Best Friend's Wedding*
3 thriller – *Psycho*
4 western – *High Noon*
5 musical – *High School Musical*
6 cartoon – *Shrek*

22.3
```
        T H R I L L E R
         H O R R O R
       C O M E D Y
          A C T I O N
S C I E N C E F I C T I O N
    W E S T E R N
    M U S I C A L
       C A R T O O N
```

22.4 **2** watched (some people say 'saw a DVD')
3 played
4 in
5 film stars
6 director

22.5 *Possible answers:*

1 I like romantic comedies.
2 My favourite film star is Nicole Kidman.
3 I prefer going to the cinema.
4 The last film I saw was *Tropic Thunder*.
5 You can look in the newspaper, go online or phone the cinema.

Unit 23

23.1
2 He's gardening.
3 He's reading a newspaper.
4 She's cooking.
5 She's using the Internet. / She's using the computer.
6 He's listening to music / a CD.

23.2
2 reading
3 talk
4 have
5 have / invite
6 play
7 download
8 see / watch
9 grows
10 watch

23.3 *Possible answers:*

1 We talk, or we have a meal, or we listen to music, etc.
2 My best friend sometimes comes to stay. / My cousins sometimes come to stay, etc.
3 I like novels, and I read a newspaper every day.
4 I talk to them on the phone every day.
5 I have an MP3 player and I use it every day.
6 I chat to my friends online once or twice a week.
7 I often download music or films from the Internet.
8 *The Sims* is my favourite computer game.
9 I use headphones when I want to listen to music on a train.

23.4 *Possible answers:*

gardening	2
cooking	4
reading	5
using the Internet	5
watching DVDs	4
listening to music	5
doing nothing	1
chatting online	2

Unit 24

24.1 2 musician   3 musical   4 music   5 musical   6 musicians

24.2
2 Patricia plays the cello in an orchestra.
3 Chunshen loves playing the drums.
4 Donna is having a piano lesson.
5 Alex is a very good trumpet-player.
6 Bethan plays the clarinet every evening.
7 William plays the guitar.
8 Emma is learning the flute. She will be a good flute-player one day.
9 Suzanna is a violinist.
10 Donna wants to be a pianist.

24.3 2 a   3 c   4 b   5 c

24.4 *Possible answers:*

1 I download music about once a month.
2 I like the violin best.
3 Yes, I play the violin and the guitar.

4 I would like to learn the piano.
5 I like classical music and pop music!

Unit 25

25.1
2 Brazil	5 Japan
3 Spain	6 Thailand
4 Morocco	

25.2
2 Rome is the capital of Italy.
3 Canberra is the capital of Australia.
4 Bogotá is the capital of Colombia.
5 Cairo is the capital of Egypt.
6 London is the capital of the UK.

7 Berlin is the capital of Germany.
8 Warsaw is the capital of Poland.
9 Buenos Aires is the capital of Argentina.
10 Madrid is the capital of Spain.

25.3
2 In Mexico, Spain and Chile they speak Spanish but in Brazil they speak Portuguese.
3 In Austria, Germany and Switzerland they speak German but in Italy they speak Italian.
4 In Morocco, Egypt and Saudi Arabia they speak Arabic but in China they speak Chinese.
5 In Switzerland, Canada and France they speak French but in Scotland they speak English.

25.4
2 Thai	7 Peruvian
3 German	8 Chinese
4 Egyptian	9 Australian
5 Argentinian	10 Polish
6 Spanish	

25.5 *Check your answers with your teacher.*

Follow-up

The Sahara is in Africa.
The Amazon is in South America.
Wagga Wagga is in Australia.
The Volga is in Europe.
Mount Kilimanjaro is in Africa.
The Mississippi is in North America.
Mount Fuji is in Asia.
Lake Titicaca is in South America.

Unit 26

26.1 2 f 3 d 4 g 5 c 6 e 7 b

26.2
3 It is windy in La Paz.
4 It is cloudy in Paris.
5 It is foggy in Tashkent.
6 It is sunny in Seoul. / The sun is shining in Seoul.
7 It is snowing in Washington. / It's snowy in Washington.

26.3
2 rains	6 degrees
3 weather	7 storm
4 snows	8 cold
5 lightning	

26.4 *Possible answers:*

2 It is usually 20 degrees in summer and 0 (zero) degrees in winter.
3 There are sometimes thunderstorms in August.
4 It is not usually very wet in spring.
5 We almost never have hurricanes.
6 Winter is my favourite season because I like snow.

26.5 *Possible answers:*

2 sunny weather – I like to go to the beach / for a walk / lie in the sun.
3 a rainy day – I don't like to go out / I don't like to do sports.
4 snow – I like to walk in the snow / I like to go skiing.
5 a windy day – I like to go windsurfing / I don't like to go out / I love to go for a walk.

Unit 27

27.1
2 at the tourist information office
3 at the bank
4 in / at the car park
5 at the museum
6 at the (train / railway) station
7 at / in the shopping centre
8 at / in the library

27.2
2 Exit
3 No smoking
4 Please do not walk on the grass
5 Entrance

27.3
2 The bus **station / stop** is over there **on** the left.
3 For the Town Hall **take** the number 14 bus.
4 **There** is a post office on the other **side** of the road.
5 You can find a cash **machine** at the bank in High Street.
6 We can get a map of the town at the tourist **information** office.
7 Can you tell me the **way** to the railway **station**, please?
8 **Excuse** me. I'm looking **for** a car park.

27.4
2 town hall
3 library
4 car park
5 railway station
6 pedestrian area
7 cash machine
8 post office
9 shops
10 bus stop

27.5 *Possible answer:*

Go left out of the tourist information office and take the first left. Then take the second left, which is Market Street. The shopping centre is on the left.

27.6 *Your own answers*

Unit 28

28.1
2 forest
3 village
4 hills
5 wood
6 farm
7 river
8 country road
9 path
10 fields
11 lake

28.2 2 cottage   3 village   4 town

28.3
2 We went walking along a five-kilometre path.
3 We went skiing down the mountain.
4 We saw some wonderful wildlife in the national park.
5 We had a picnic sitting by the river.

28.4   2 He loves nature.   3 She wants to live in the country.   4 They are interested in wildlife.

28.5 *Possible answers:*

2 There are no hills or mountains.
3 There's a big lake and two small rivers.
4 There are a lot of villages and some small towns.
5 There are a lot of small farms and a few very big ones in the countryside.
6 There are some good paths for walking near where I live.
7 You can't go skiing because there are no hills (and there's usually no snow).
8 You can see a lot of beautiful wildlife.

Unit 29

29.1 *Possible answers:*

2 giraffe	7 Chickens / hens
3 Parrots; hens	8 Rabbits
4 Tigers; lions	9 feed; give
5 horse; elephant	10 take
6 Fish; birds	

29.2

sheep	lamb	lamb
cow	beef	calf
hen	chicken	chick
pig	pork	piglet

29.3 *Possible answers:*

1 Lions, tigers, monkeys, snakes, dogs and cats eat meat.
2 Cows, sheep, pigs, goats, parrots (for feathers) and snakes (for snakeskin) give us things that we wear.
3 Chickens / hens, tortoises, parrots, snakes and fish produce their babies in eggs.
4 We can eat cows, sheep, pigs, chickens / hens, goats, horses and fish (and you may think of some other animals that people eat too).

29.4

Across	Down
3 cats	1 parrot
6 lion	2 monkey
7 horse	4 sheep
8 elephant	5 tiger
	9 hen

29.5 Write down the number you remembered. Try again tomorrow and write down how many you remember then.

Unit 30

30.1 2 d   3 a   4 f   5 c   6 g   7 b

30.2 2 True.
3 False. Planes take off at the beginning of a journey. / Planes land at the end of a journey.
4 False. You need a boarding card to get on a plane.
5 False. Hiring a car is not the same as buying a car.
6 True.

30.3 *Possible answer:*

At Cambridge train station take a number 5 bus. The stop is just outside the station. Get off the bus at the hospital, cross the road and take the first road on the left. My house is on the corner of the street and it has a red door.

30.4

Across	Down
3 map	1 timetable
6 helicopter	2 taxi
7 bus	3 motorcycle
8 petrol	4 platform
	5 train

Follow-up

Keep the cards and test yourself every day. If you find this useful, write cards for words from other units of the book.

Unit 31

31.1
2 Christmas   5 Valentine's Day
3 Bonfire Night   6 New Year's Eve / Hogmanay
4 Easter

31.2

C	H	I	C	K	E	N	F	D	K	N
R	Y	O	R	K	S	H	I	R	E	P
O	C	V	O	M	T	R	S	M	V	U
A	Q	E	W	A	A	T	H	X	L	D
S	M	V	C	S	H	G	E	Q	L	D
T	P	O	T	A	T	O	E	S	C	I
D	F	G	B	L	B	K	U	V	U	N
X	Z	O	E	A	P	I	V	Z	R	G
A	N	D	E	C	H	I	P	S	R	B
C	W	Q	F	T	I	K	K	A	Y	J

31.3
2 India   4 No. They eat it with their main course (with roast beef).
3 curry   5 in the oven

31.4
2 a state secondary school   4 a state primary school
3 a nursery school   5 a private secondary school

31.5 *Answers in 2009:*

1 Gordon Brown   2 Houses of Parliament   3 Queen Elizabeth II

Unit 32

32.1
2 a murderer   5 a mugger
3 a shoplifter / robber   6 a drug dealer
4 a burglar

32.2
2 arrested   6 innocent
3 vandals   7 terrorists
4 fine   8 prison
5 burglaries / burglars

32.3   2 False – vandals destroy things   3 True   4 False – a car thief steals cars   5 True

32.4   2 stole   3 robbed   4 stolen   5 stole   6 stolen

Follow-up

Possible answers:

2 The student should pay a fine and return the book.
3 The woman should go to prison.
4 The terrorists should go to prison for a long time.
5 The woman should pay a fine and the police should take her car away.
6 The teenager should work in the park and plant new trees or pay a fine.

Unit 33

33.1
2 is	6 online
3 documentary	7 change
4 nature	8 interview
5 teenage	

33.2 2 e   3 b   4 a   5 d   6 c

33.3
2 a journalist	6 an advert / advertisement
3 an evening (news)paper	7 a (TV) channel
4 a cartoon	8 an interview
5 a nature programme	

33.4 *Possible answers:*

1 I always read an evening newspaper.
2 I like news magazines.
3 I'll probably watch my favourite soap on TV tonight.
4 My favourite TV channel is BBC1.
5 I watch about an hour of TV every day.
6 I like talk shows and reality TV.
7 I watch TV online once or twice a week.
8 No, I don't like watching adverts on TV.

Unit 34

34.1 *Possible answers:*

2 The computer has crashed.	6 He's cut his hand.
3 The cup is broken.	7 The room is untidy.
4 The phone is out of order.	8 She is late for work.
5 She has too much work (to do).	

34.2 *Possible answers:*

2 cut finger / hands / knees
3 untidy room / desk / hair
4 late for school / an appointment / a concert
5 a camera / microwave / MP3 player that isn't working
6 too much work / rain / wind

34.3 *Possible answers:*

2 dying plants   2
3 a cut finger   2
4 being late for work or school   1
5 a colleague or friend in a bad mood   2
6 a coffee machine that isn't working   1
7 a broken washing machine   1
8 an untidy bedroom   3
9 a row with a friend   1
10 your computer crashes   1
11 lost keys   1
12 too much work   3

34.4 *Possible answers:*

too much work – get an assistant
a colleague in a bad mood – pay no attention
a crashed computer – get a technician
a photocopier that is out of order – repair the photocopier
a coffee machine that isn't working – drink water

34.5 *Possible answers:*

My DVD player didn't work.
My brother lost his credit card.
I cut my knee.
My cousin broke a glass.

Unit 35

35.1
2 car crash
3 flood
4 war
5 earthquake
6 forest fire
7 hurricane
8 traffic jam
9 snowstorm

35.2
2 traffic jam
3 rush hour
4 forest fire
5 crowded cities
6 homeless people
7 car crash
8 earthquake

35.3
2 a traffic jam
3 crowded
4 a car crash
5 unemployed
6 the rush hour
7 hungry
8 a forest fire

35.4 *Possible answers:*

2 forest fire, traffic jam
3 strike, war
4 hurricane, snowstorm, flood
5 poor, hungry, homeless, unemployed

35.5
2 strike
3 War
4 car crash
5 earthquakes; snowstorms
6 homeless
7 rush hour
8 polluted

Unit 36

36.1 *Possible answers:*

2 lesson
3 football / tennis / squash / rugby / darts / chess / cards
4 party
5 shower / bath / wash
6 exam
7 meeting
8 coffee / cup of coffee / cup of tea / drink
9 swim
10 dinner / a meal / supper / something to eat

36.2
2 Nadia has gone to the hairdresser's to **have her hair cut**.
3 That computer game looks great. Can I have a **go**?
4 I want to have **a word** with my teacher after the lesson.
5 Mum didn't have the **time** to go to the shop today.
6 They **don't have** *or* they **haven't got** any cake in the café today.

36.3

¹m	²e	a	l	
	x			
³p	a	r	⁴t	y
	m	■	e	
	⁵g	a	m	e

36.4 *Possible answers:*

2 Have a good journey! / Have a good time!
3 Have you got a cold?
4 Can I have a look?

36.5 *Possible answers:*

1 I've got one brother and two sisters.
2 I have them at 9.30 every day.
3 I have a salad and a cup of tea.
4 Not every day, but I have to go on Wednesday and Friday.
5 I've got two.
6 Yes, we always have a good time in our English classes.

Unit 37

37.1
2 The Sharps are going to the beach.
3 Lili and Karl are going shopping / to the shopping centre.
4 Imran is going to Cairo.
5 Jan is going fishing.

37.2
2 This year Alison is going to pass her driving test.
3 This year Alison is going to learn Spanish.
4 This year Alison is going to watch less TV.
5 This year Alison is going to keep her room tidy.

37.3 *Possible answers:*

I sometimes go swimming.
I never go skiing.
I sometimes go dancing.
I never go fishing.
I always go sightseeing.

37.4 *Possible answers:*

From Cambridge, trains go to London, Norwich, Ely and Peterborough. Buses go to Oxford, to Heathrow and to Scotland from Cambridge. From Cambridge roads go to London, to Huntingdon and to the sea.

37.5 2 Mum is **going shopping** this afternoon.
 3 ✓
 4 I love Paris. Did you **go there** last year?
 5 Milos is **going home** at 4 o'clock.
 6 We always go to the same café. Let's **go somewhere** different today.
 7 ✓
 8 I **go swimming** every Sunday morning.
 9 We're going **sightseeing** today.
 10 Jo went **up** to the top of the hill. / Jo went down to the **bottom** of the hill.
 11 Let's go **fishing** today.
 12 She went out **of** the shop.
 13 ✓
 14 Would you like to **go home** now?

Unit 38

38.1 2 What are the girls doing? They're playing tennis.
 3 What is the dog doing? It's sleeping.
 4 What is the man in the house doing? He's washing up. / He's doing the washing-up.
 5 What is the woman doing? She's reading a book.
 6 What is the man in the garden doing? He's gardening. / He's doing the gardening.

38.2 *Questions and possible answers:*

 2 What does Lara Brown do? She's a secretary.
 3 What does Sophie Hicks do? She's a doctor.
 4 What do Jo and Ted do? They're students.

38.3 2 What did Lara Brown do? She went to a meeting.
 3 What did Sophie Hicks do? She talked to five patients.
 4 What did Jo and Ted do? They wrote an essay.

38.4 *Possible answers:*

I often do the washing-up.
My husband usually does the washing.
My son has to do his homework every day.
My daughter does her exercises every morning.
I hate doing the housework.
I love doing the gardening.
We do business with Eastern Europe.
I always do my best.

38.5 ANNA: Where did you **go** on your holidays? To London?
 PAVEL: No, we **didn't** go to London this year. We went to Scotland.
 ANNA: **Does** your grandmother **live** in Scotland?
 PAVEL: No, she **doesn't** but my uncle **does**.

Unit 39

39.1   2 made   5 made / have made / 've made
         3 making   6 making
         4 make

39.2   2 Long lessons always make me (feel) tired.
         3 She was horrible to me; it made me (feel) angry.
         4 It's a lovely song. It makes me (feel) happy.
         5 That meal was horrible. It made me (feel) sick.

39.3   2 She's making tea.   5 The children are making a mess.
         3 The children are making a noise.   6 The girl is making her bed.
         4 They're making a video / a film.

39.4   2 Can I **take** a photo of you?
         3 He's 25 but he never **does** his own washing. He takes his dirty clothes to his mother's.
         4 Are you **doing / taking** an exam tomorrow?
         5 Have you **done** your homework yet?

Unit 40

40.1   2 back (home)   5 see
         3 into   6 out of / back from / home from
         4 from

40.2   2 Come here!
         3 We're going to a party. Do you want to come along?
         4 I come from France.

40.3   2 came   3 comes   4 Are; coming   5 comes

40.4   *Possible answers:*

1 I usually come home at five-thirty.
2 I'm from / I come from Scotland / Jamaica / Pakistan / Latvia / Bolivia, etc.
3 I sit down and talk to my friends / take out my books.

Follow-up

Possible meanings and example sentences:
1 Meaning: 'come round' can mean 'come to someone's house or flat'.
   Example: Do you want to come round this afternoon for a coffee?
2 Meaning: 'come across' can mean 'meet or find for the first time'.
   Example: I come across lots of new words when I read English books.
3 Meaning: 'come up' can mean 'be mentioned or occur in conversation'.
   Example: When new words come up in class, the teacher tells us the meaning.

Unit 41

41.1   *Possible answers:*

1 It takes me 10 minutes to get to university.
2 It takes me 30 minutes to go from my house to the nearest railway station.
3 It takes me 20 minutes to get to my best friend's house.
4 It takes me an hour to do one unit of this book.

41.2   2 take the train   3 take a course   4 take some water

41.3   2 You can / have to take a taxi.   3 He takes the bus.   4 They take the underground.

41.4   2 I take my / an umbrella.   4 I take my books and pens / pencils.
            3 I take my passport.   5 I take my mobile (phone).

41.5   *Possible answer:*

       It took me about an hour.

Unit 42

42.1   2 bring   3 bring   4 Take   5 take   6 bring

42.2   2 e You must take your passport when you travel.
            3 b Come to my house and bring your guitar.
            4 a Go to the post office and take these letters, please.
            5 d Everybody is going to bring food to the party.

42.3   1 brings; brought   2 brought   3 take   4 take; bring

42.4   1 take; bring it back   2 brought me back   3 take; bring it back

42.5   *Possible answer:*

       I always bring / take my vocabulary notebook, a pen and my coursebook to the lesson.

Unit 43

43.1   2 c sick   4 b dark
            3 a hot   5 c wet

43.2   2 When the sun comes up it gets light.   4 It's raining! I'm getting wet!
            3 She's in hospital but she's getting better.   5 Please close the window. I'm getting cold.

43.3   2 a doctor
            3 a drink
            4 a pen / pencil and paper
            5 a newspaper
            6 a taxi / a bus / a train
            7 a job
            8 an umbrella / a raincoat

43.4   2 gets to   3 get to   4 gets (back)   5 get back / home

43.5   *Possible answers:*

       1 In Britain, people usually get married when they are 20 to 30 years old.
       2 People usually get married at the weekend, mostly on Saturday. April, May and June are very
          popular months (spring and summer).
       3 I get home at about 5 o'clock. I get there by car.

Unit 44

44.1   2 d   3 g   4 f   5 b   6 h   7 e   8 a

44.2   2 off   3 on; up   4 off   5 off   6 off   7 on   8 on

44.3   2 He is putting on his shoes.   3 A plane is taking off.   4 She is turning on the oven.

44.4   2 took off   3 went on   4 went off   5 turned down

Unit 45

45.1   2 She washes (the / her) clothes every Saturday.   4 He watches TV / television every evening.
            3 He cleans the house / his flat every weekend.   5 She goes for a walk every Sunday.

45.2 *Possible questions:*

2 How often do you go for a walk?
3 How do you go to work?
4 When do you have dinner?
5 How do you come home from work?

6 How often do you phone your best friend?
7 When do you clean your room?
8 What time do you have a shower?

45.3 *Possible answers:*

1 I usually wake up at 7 o'clock.
2 I go to the bathroom and have a shower.
3 I usually have tea and toast for breakfast.
4 I go to work by car.
5 I usually have a cup of coffee at 11 o'clock.
6 I usually come home at about 6 pm.
7 I usually make dinner at 7 o'clock.
8 In the evenings I normally watch TV or go for a walk.
9 Sometimes I write a letter or email or listen to the radio.
10 I usually go to bed at 11 o'clock.

Unit 46

46.1 2 told   3 said   4 tell; said   5 said   6 told

46.2 2 How do you say 'tree' in German?
3 Excuse me, can you tell me the time?
4 I just want to say goodbye (to you).
5 Can you tell me when the exam is?
6 Can you answer the phone, please? / Can you tell them I'm busy / I'm cooking?

46.3 2 h   answer the door
3 g   ask for the bill
4 a   reply to a letter
5 f   tell someone a joke
6 e   talk to a friend
7 b   ask someone to help you
8 c   speak Japanese

We can also say 'answer a letter', but not 'reply to the door'!

46.4 2 Can we have the bill, please?
3 Happy New Year!
4 Tell me a story before I go to sleep. Please!

Unit 47

47.1 2 danced   4 run   6 fell   8 walk
3 swims   5 climbing   7 jumped; swam

47.2 2 drives   6 ride
3 takes   7 ride
4 drives   8 take
5 take; go by

Note: You can also use 'go by' with all these forms of transport (but without 'the' or 'a'),
i.e. you can go to work by bicycle, go home by underground / taxi, etc.

47.3 *Possible answers:*

salt, pepper, bread, butter, water, sauce, salad

47.4   2 Maria drove her grandmother to the city yesterday.
3 Bill flew to Madrid yesterday.
4 I took a taxi home from the station yesterday.
5 Jane fell when she rode her bike yesterday.
6 Paul missed the 7.30 bus to school yesterday.
7 The taxi driver helped the old lady to carry her luggage to the train yesterday.
8 Susie danced very well yesterday.

47.5   *Possible answers:*

2 I ride my bike once a week.
3 I swim in the sea once a year. I swim in a pool once a week.
4 I go somewhere by plane once a year.
5 I drive my car every day.
6 I go dancing once a week.
7 I never go climbing.
8 I take a taxi once or twice a year.

Unit 48

48.1   Check your work with your teacher if you are not sure about your answers.

48.2

noun	verb	adjective
book	speak	good
word	have	new
house	write	right
man	say	blue

48.3   *Possible answers:*

on, at, by, to, for, with, below

48.4   2 question   5 question
3 phrase   6 sentence
4 sentence

48.5   2 man   6 No, it's an adjective. The adverb is badly.
3 No, it's a preposition.   7 They are both pronouns.
4 No, it's a noun.   8 because
5 No, it's a sentence.

48.6   Nouns: cat, garden, day, milk
Adjective: fresh
Adverb: happily
Preposition: in
Pronoun: She

Unit 49

49.1   2 and   4 so   6 if   8 when
3 before   5 because   7 or

49.2 *Possible sentences:*

Mary agreed to marry Sanjay after he moved to London. / Mary agreed to marry Sanjay after they decided to set up a business together.
Mary agreed to marry Sanjay and they had two sons. / Mary agreed to marry Sanjay and they decided to set up a business together.
Mary agreed to marry Sanjay because she loved him. / Mary agreed to marry Sanjay because he was a pop star.
Mary agreed to marry Sanjay before he moved to London. / Mary agreed to marry Sanjay before they decided to set up a business together.
Mary will marry Sanjay because she loves him.
Mary will marry Sanjay before he moves to London.
Mary will marry Sanjay but she doesn't love him.
Mary agreed to marry Sanjay if he moved to London.
Mary will marry Sanjay or she won't marry anyone.
Mary agreed to marry Sanjay so he moved to London.
Mary will marry Sanjay when he moves to London.

49.3 2 as well / also (too is also possible but it is better to use a different word as too is already in the sentence)
3 than
4 like
5 only

49.4 *Possible answers:*

I only play tennis in the summer.
My sister plays the piano better than I do.
My brother swims like a fish.
I like listening to music and I like reading also.
I like going skiing too.
I often go skiing with the children and sometimes my husband comes as well.

49.5 *Possible answers:*

1 I'm learning English because I enjoy it.
2 I'll learn more English if I do all the exercises in this book.
3 I'm learning English and I'm also studying Spanish.
4 I started learning English when I was ten.
5 I can speak some English, so it's OK on holiday in the UK.
6 I'll learn more English but sometimes it's difficult.

Unit 50

50.1 2 a century   3 a fortnight   4 an hour   5 a week

50.2 Thirty days has September,
April, June and November.
All the rest have thirty-one.
Except for February
Which has twenty-eight days
And twenty-nine in each leap year.

This is a traditional rhyme which people use to help them remember the number of days of the month. It means that:
September, April, June and November have 30 days. The other months have 31 days except for February which has 28 days and 29 days in a leap year.

50.3 2 August   5 Wednesday   8 Friday   11 Tuesday
      3 October   6 January   9 February   12 November
      4 Saturday 7 April   10 September

50.4 2 T F S (the first letters of the days of the week)
      3 A S O N D (the first letters of the months)

50.5 I'm going to a party on **Saturday** for Jill's birthday. Her birthday is on **Thursday** but
      she wanted to have the party **at** the weekend. She's having a barbecue. I think **June** is a
      good month to have a birthday because of the weather. I love going to barbecues **in** the
      summer. My birthday is in **winter** and it's too cold to eat outside!

50.6 1 15   2 Tuesday (*or* Wednesday)   3 300   4 July   5 120
      6–12   It is not possible to give answers to questions 6 to 12. Check with your teacher if
         you are not sure if your answers are correct or not.

Unit 51

51.1 2 for   3 from   4 to   5 At   6 for

51.2 2 the 22nd century – the future   4 the 21st century – the present
      3 the 18th century – the past   5 the 20th century – the past

51.3 *Possible answers:*

      2 I sometimes go to school by bus. I usually go by car.
      3 I often watch TV.
      4 I never drink milk. I usually drink coffee.
      5 I never wear a hat.
      6 I often eat chocolate.
      7 I sometimes go to bed at 10. I usually go to bed at 11.
      8 I sometimes go to the theatre.

51.4 2 Probably a week ago   3 In a few minutes   4 4 o'clock

51.5 John plays tennis twice a week. He practises the piano once a week and he has a business
      meeting in Germany once a month.
      Bettina and Amy play tennis three times a week. They practise the piano twice a day.
      They go to Germany for a business meeting six times a year. *or* They have a business
      meeting in Germany six times a year.

Unit 52

52.1 2 here   3 there   4 everywhere   5 there   6 back

52.2 2 at   3 on   4 at   5 on   6 in; in

52.3
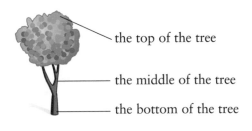
the back of the bus

the side of the bus

the front of the bus

the top of the tree

the middle of the tree

the bottom of the tree

52.4 2 out   3 away   4 away; abroad

52.5 *Possible answers:*

1 I'm studying English in the UK.
2 Yes, I'm going to Dublin and to the US.
3 At the moment I have a pen in my right hand.
4 The Answer key is at the end of this book.
5 Unit 3 is at the beginning of this book (Unit 3 out of 60 units). (*Note:* we say *at.*)
6 Unit 36 is in the middle of this book (Unit 36 out of 60 units). (*Note:* we say *in.*)

Unit 53

53.1 2 badly 3 loudly 4 fast [NOT ~~fastly~~] 5 quietly 6 well

53.2 2 slow 3 good 4 in 5 right 6 badly 7 quietly 8 the

53.3 suddenly ✗ sadly ✓ strangely ✓ quickly ✗ easily ✓
Suddenly means very quickly, when you are not expecting it.
Quickly is similar to 'fast' when fast is an adverb, not when it is an adjective.

53.4 *Possible answers:*

2 My brother speaks German badly.
3 I usually eat too fast.
4 My dog is old and very slow.
5 My voice is quiet.

6 I like to sing loudly.
7 My Mum always behaves in a friendly way.
8 I like to do things the right way.

Unit 54

54.1 2 milk; butter 3 advice 4 air 5 work 6 traffic

54.2 2 useful information 4 modern furniture 6 cold water
3 bad news 5 brown bread 7 space travel

54.3 2 is / was 3 is / was 4 is; was 5 is / was 6 is / was

54.4 2 Where can I get some **information** about your country?
3 Let me give you **some** advice.
4 Cook **this** spaghetti for ten minutes.
5 Can I have **some** bread, please?
6 We need to buy some new **furniture**.
7 The east of the country usually has better weather than the west. [NOT ~~a~~ better weather]
8 I must find **some** new accommodation soon.

Unit 55

55.1 *Possible answers:*

2 very bad / terrible / awful / dreadful
3 terrible / awful / dreadful
4 excellent / great / wonderful
5 awful / horrible

6 wonderful / lovely
7 bad
8 wonderful / lovely

55.2 *Possible answers:*

2 Oh, how awful!
3 That's a lovely idea! / Yes, great!
4 Yes, there's the Ritz. It's an excellent restaurant.

5 They're wonderful!
6 Yes, that's perfect!

55.3 2 e 3 d 4 a 5 b

55.4

good	bad
brilliant marvellous fine	dreadful nasty

55.5 *Possible answers:*

brilliant idea / scientist   nasty surprise / smell
marvellous weather / food   fine weather / day

Unit 56

56.1   2 horrible   3 kind   4 naughty   5 selfish

56.2   2 wonderful   3 lovely   4 difficult   5 nice   6 easy-going   7 horrible

56.3   *Your own answers*

56.4   2 of   3 to   4 of

Unit 57

57.1   2 d   This bicycle belongs to the hotel.
        3 h   The children thanked their aunt for the money.
        4 g   Sally is listening to her MP3 player.
        5 a   He apologised for his mistake.
        6 e   Let me pay for our tickets.
        7 b   Hamid is thinking about the holidays.
        8 f   Over 100 people came to the football match.

57.2   2 after people   4 forward to my party   6 for a new one   8 after the children
        3 for them   5 at me   7 forward to it

57.3   2 at   3 to   4 in   5 to   6 of   7 about   8 to

57.4   3 Hiroshi wasn't used to eating British food.   5 He was used to expensive shops.
        4 He was used to traffic jams.   6 He wasn't used to British money.

57.5   *Possible answers:*

     1 I was good at languages and bad at PE.   5 I like listening to folk music.
     2 I usually ask for a black coffee.   6 I am looking forward to my holiday.
     3 I am proud of my family.   7 I belong to a tennis club.
     4 I am afraid of going to the dentist.   8 I am used to eating lots of different kinds of food.

Unit 58

58.1   2 rewrite / redo   3 informal   4 unhappy   5 half-price   6 unsafe

58.2   *Possible answers:*

     2 An ex-president is giving a lecture here tomorrow.   4 It's impossible to read his handwriting.
     3 This work is not very good. Please redo it.   5 Pre-school children learn by playing.

58.3 2 nerves before an exam
   3 a wrong answer, an answer that is not correct
   4 a book that has not been read
   5 to tell a story again
   6 a brother with one parent the same (for example, perhaps with the same mother but not the same father)
   7 a letter that is not finished
   8 a drink with no alcohol in it (for example, fruit juice, cola)
   9 to read a book again
   10 to send an email again

58.4 2 uncomfortable   3 impolite   4 unpleasant   5 unattractive

Follow-up

Possible answers:

in: This is an incomplete answer – you need to finish it.
im: I thought the question he asked me was very impolite.
non: I want to buy a non-stick pan.
pre: Would you like to have a pre-lunch drink?
re: We're going to repaint this room next week.
un: My daughter's room is always very untidy.

Unit 59

59.1 2 instructor   3 swimmer   4 happily   5 calculator   6 useful

59.2 *Possible answers:*

You may be able to think of some other possible combinations.
   2 fast worker / car / swimmer
   3 beautiful beach / weather / car / book / smile / picture
   4 sandy beach
   5 sunny weather / smile
   6 hard worker
   7 useful idea / book
   8 endless fun
   9 useless idea / book (*Note:* You can also say 'I'm a useless swimmer'. It is typical of spoken rather than written English and means 'I am no good at swimming'.)

59.3 2 badly   3 helpful   4 kindness   5 careless   6 windy   7 easily   8 builder

59.4 2 a person who travels   7 the opposite of doing something well
   3 the opposite of fast   8 a thing for opening tins
   4 with lots of hope   9 a person who plays football
   5 weather when it is raining   10 weather when there is a lot of snow
   6 it doesn't hurt

Unit 60

60.1 2 lose   3 felt   4 cooker   5 fell   6 quite   7 loose   8 cook

60.2 2 loose – *juice*   3 quite – *right*   4 quiet – *higher*

60.3 2 He/She checks it.   4 Good afternoon.   6 Can you lend me £1?
   3 Can I borrow your camera?   5 They wait for the bus.   7 Please be quiet.

60.4 *Possible answers:*

   1 I am expecting my brother at 5.30. (= He said he would come at 5.30.)
   2 I hope to go on holiday to Spain. (= I really want to go to Spain.)
   3 Sometimes I borrow books and CDs.
   4 Yes, but only to my best friend!

Phonemic symbols

Vowel sounds

Symbol	Examples
/iː/	sleep me
/i/	happy recipe
/ɪ/	pin dinner
/ʊ/	foot could pull
/uː/	do shoe through
/e/	red head said
/ə/	arrive father colour
/ɜː/	turn bird work
/ɔː/	sort thought walk
/ae/	cat black
/ʌ/	sun enough wonder
/ɒ/	got watch sock
/ɑː/	part heart laugh
/eɪ/	name late aim
/aɪ/	my idea time
/ɔɪ/	boy noise
/eə/	pair where bear
/ɪə/	hear beer
/əʊ/	go home show
/aʊ/	out cow
/ʊə/	pure fewer

Consonant sounds

Symbol	Examples
/p/	put
/b/	book
/t/	take
/d/	dog
/k/	car kick
/g/	go guarantee
/tʃ/	catch church
/dʒ/	age lounge
/f/	for cough photograph
/v/	love vehicle
/θ/	thick path
/ð/	this mother
/s/	since rice
/z/	zoo houses
/ʃ/	shop sugar machine
/ʒ/	pleasure usual vision
/h/	hear hotel
/m/	make
/n/	name now know
/ŋ/	bring
/l/	look while
/r/	road
/j/	young
/w/	wear

' This shows that the next syllable is the one with the stress.

, This is used when some longer words have a second stress, less strong than on the main stressed syllable.

Index

The numbers in the Index are **Unit** numbers not page numbers. The pronunciation provided is for standard British English.

fall asleep fɔːl əˈsliːp 12
family ˈfæmli 1
farm fɑːm 28
farm animal fɑːm ˈænɪməl 29
farmer ˈfɑːmə 14, 28
fast fɑːst 53
fast food fɑːst fuːd 10
fast food restaurant fɑːst fuːd ˈrestrɒn 20
fat fæt 5
father ˈfɑːðə 1
favourite ˈfeɪvərɪt 21, 33
February ˈfebruəri 50
feed fiːd 29
feel fiːl 6, 60
feelings ˈfiːlɪŋz 7
feet fiːt 3
ferry ˈferi 17
field ˈfiːld 28
fill in a form fɪl ɪn ə fɔːm 19
fill up with fɪl ʌp wɪð 30
film fɪlm 22
film star fɪlm stɑː 22
fine faɪn 6, 32
finger ˈfɪŋgə 3
Finnish ˈfɪnɪʃ 25
fireworks ˈfaɪəwɜːks 31
first floor ˈfɜːst flɔː 18
fish fɪʃ 10, 20, 29
fish and chips fɪʃ ənd tʃɪps 10, 20, 31
flight flaɪt 17, 30
flight attendant flaɪt əˈtendənt 30
flood flʌd 35
floor flɔː 18
flute fluːt 24
flute-player fluːt ˈpleɪə 24
fly flaɪ 17, 47
foal fəʊl 29
fog fɒg 26
foggy ˈfɒgi 26
folk music fəʊk ˈmjuːzɪk 24
food fuːd 10, 7, 18
foot fʊt 3
football ˈfʊtbɔːl 21
football hooligan ˈfʊtbɔːl ˈhuːlɪgən 32
football hooliganism ˈfʊtbɔːl ˈhuːlɪgənɪzəm 32
forest ˈfɒrɪst 28

forest fire ˈfɒrɪst faɪə 35
fork fɔːk 11
form fɔːm 19
fortnight ˈfɔːtnaɪt 50
fourth fɔːθ 18
freezer ˈfriːzə 11
Friday ˈfraɪdeɪ 50
fridge frɪdʒ 11
friend frend 23
friendly ˈfrendli 53
front frʌnt 52
fruit fruːt 10
fruit juice fruːt dʒuːs 10
fruit salad fruːt ˈsæləd 20
frying pan ˈfraɪɪŋ pæn 11
funeral ˈfjuːnərəl 2
furniture ˈfɜːnɪtʃə 18, 54
future ˈfjuːtʃə 51
game geɪm 36
gardening ˈgɑːdənɪŋ 23
garlic ˈgɑːlɪk 10
geography dʒiˈɒgrəfi 15
German ˈdʒɜːmən 25
Germany ˈdʒɜːməni 25
get get 43
get a degree get ə dɪˈgriː 15
get back get bæk 43
get dressed get drest 4
get home get həʊm 43
get married get ˈmærid 2, 43
get off get ɒf 44
get on get ɒn 44
get to get tə 43
get undressed get ʌnˈdrest 4
get up get ʌp 12, 44, 45
gift shop gɪft ʃɒp 18
giraffe dʒɪˈrɑːf 29
give gɪv 29
give a lift gɪv ə lɪft 30
glass glɑːs 11
glasses ˈglɑːsɪz 4
global ˈgləʊbəl 35
gloves glʌvz 4
go gəʊ 12, 21, 22, 37, 40
go by gəʊ baɪ 37, 47
go dancing gəʊ ˈdɑːntsɪŋ 37
go down gəʊ daʊn 37
go fishing gəʊ ˈfɪʃɪŋ 37
go for a walk gəʊ fɔːr ə wɔːk 45

go in gəʊ ɪn 37
go into gəʊ ˈɪntə 37
go off gəʊ ɒf 44
go on gəʊ ɒn 44
go out of gəʊ aʊt ɒv 37
go shopping gəʊ ˈʃɒpɪŋ 37
go sightseeing gəʊ ˈsaɪtsiːɪŋ 37
go skiing gəʊ ˈskiːɪŋ 37
go swimming gəʊ ˈswɪmɪŋ 37
go through gəʊ θruː 30
go to bed gəʊ tə bed 45
go to the bathroom gəʊ tə ðə ˈbɑːθrum 45
go to work gəʊ tə wɜːk 45
go up gəʊ ʌp 37
goat gəʊt 29
goatskin ˈgəʊtskɪn 29
going to ˈgəʊɪŋ tuː 37
good gʊd 53, 55, 56
good afternoon gʊd ˌɑːftəˈnuːn 8
good at gʊd æt 57
good evening gʊd ˈiːvnɪŋ 8
good for somebody gʊd fə ˈsʌmbədi 6
good luck gʊd lʌk 8
good morning gʊdˈmɔːnɪŋ 8
goodbye gʊdˈbaɪ 8, 46
good-looking ˌgʊdˈlʊkɪŋ 5
goodnight ˌgʊdˈnaɪt 8
granddaughter ˈgrænˌdɔːtə 1
grandfather ˈgrænˌfɑːðə 1
grandmother ˈgrænˌmʌðə 1
grandparents ˈgrænˌpeərənts 1
grandson ˈgrænsʌn 1
grape(s) greɪp 10
great greɪt 55
green griːn 5
green beans griːn biːnz 20
greetings ˈgriːtɪŋz 8
groom gruːm 2
ground floor graʊnd flɔː 18
grow flowers / vegetables grəʊ flaʊəz / ˈvedʒtəbəlz 23
guilty ˈgɪlti 32

guitar gɪ'tɑː 24
hair heə 3, 5, 29
hairbrush 'heəbrʌʃ 12
hairdresser('s) 'heə‚dresə 14
hairdryer 'heə‚draɪə 19
half hɑːf 58
half-brother 'hɑːf‚brʌðə 58
half-price ‚hɑːf'praɪs 58
Halloween ‚hæləʊ'iːn 31
ham hæm 29
hamburger 'hæm‚bɜːgə 10
hand hænd 3
handbag 'hænbæg 4
happily 'hæpɪli 59
happiness 'hæpɪnəs 59
happy 'hæpi 7, 56
happy about 'hæpi ə'baʊt 7, 57
Happy Birthday 'hæpi 'bɜːθdeɪ 8, 46
Happy Christmas 'hæpi 'krɪsməs 8
happy for 'hæpi fɔː 7
Happy New Year 'hæpi njuː jɪə 8, 46
hat hæt 4
hate heɪt 7
have hæv 12, 20, 23, 36
have (your) hair cut hæv heə kʌt 36
have a baby hæv ə 'beɪbi 2
have a bad day hæv ə bæd deɪ 34
have a cold hæv ə kəʊld 36
have a cup of tea (coffee) hæv ə kʌp əv tiː 20
have a go hæv ə gəʊ 36
have a good journey hæv ə gʊd 'dʒɜːni 36
have a good time hæv ə gʊd taɪm 36
have a great time hæv ə greɪt taɪm 17
have a headache hæv ə 'hedeɪk 36
have a healthy diet hæv ə 'helθi daɪət 6
have a heart attack hæv ə hɑːt ə'tæk 6
have a lesson hæv ə 'lesən 36
have a look hæv ə lʊk 36

have a meal hæv ə miːl 36
have a meeting hæv ə 'miːtɪŋ 36
have a moment hæv ə 'məʊmənt 36
have a party hæv ə 'pɑːti 36
have a picnic hæv ə 'pɪknɪk 28
have a row with hæv ə raʊ wɪð 34
have a shower hæv ə ʃaʊə 45
have a word with hæv ə wɜːd wɪð 36
have an exam hæv æn ɪg'zæm 36
have breakfast hæv 'brekfəst 36, 45
have coffee hæv 'kɒfi 36
have dinner hæv 'dɪnə 36
have friends round hæv frendz raʊnd 23
have got hæv gɒt 36
have got … on hæv gɒt ɒn 4
have lunch hæv lʌnʃ 36
have the time hæv ðə taɪm 36
have to hæv tuː 36
Have you got any …? hæv juː gɒt 'eni 1
hay fever heɪ 'fiːvə 6
head hed 3, 5
headache 'hedeɪk 6
headphones 'hedfəʊnz 23
health helθ 6
heart hɑːt 3
heart attack hɑːt ə'tæk 6
heavy 'hevi 5
height haɪt 5
helicopter 'helɪkɒptə 30
hello hel'əʊ 8, 46
hen hen 29
here hɪə 52
here is … hɪər ɪz 19
hi haɪ 8
hi-fi 'haɪfaɪ 13
hill hɪl 28
hip hɪp 3
hire haɪə 30
history 'hɪstri 15
hobby 'hɒbi 23
holiday 'hɒlədeɪ 17

home həʊm 12, 23, 34, 52
homeless 'həʊmləs 35
homework 'həʊmwɜːk 15, 36
honeymoon 'hʌnimuːn 2
hooligan 'huːlɪgən 32
hope həʊp 7, 60
horrible 'hɒrəbəl 55, 56
horror 'hɒrə 22
horse hɔːs 29
horse racing 'hɔːs ‚reɪsɪŋ 21
hospital 'hɒspɪtəl 14
hot hɒt 7, 26
hot dog hɒt dɒg 10
hotel həʊ'tel 19
hour aʊə 50
Houses of Parliament 'haʊzɪz əv 'pɑːləmənt 31
How (awful) haʊ 55
How about …? haʊ ə'baʊt 7, 9
How are you? haʊ ə juː 6, 8
How do I get to …? haʊ duː aɪ get tə 27
How do you …? haʊ duː juː 45
How do you say …? haʊ duː juː seɪ 46
How long does it take …? haʊ lɒŋ dəz ɪt teɪk 41
How much …? haʊ mʌtʃ 19
How often do you …? haʊ 'ɒfən də juː 45
How would you like …? haʊ wʊd juː laɪk 20
hungry 'hʌŋgri 7, 35
hurricane 'hʌrɪkən 26, 35
hurry up 'hʌri ʌp 9
husband 'hʌzbənd 1
I don't mind aɪ dəʊnt maɪnd 9
I'd like … aɪd laɪk 20
I'll have … aɪl hæv 20
ice cream ‚aɪs'kriːm 36
ICT (information communication technology) ‚aɪsiː'tiː 15
if ɪf 49
ill ɪl 2, 6, 7
illness 'ɪlnəs 6
impossible ɪm'pɒsəbəl 58

in ɪn 22, 47, 52
in a bad mood ɪn ə bæd
 muːd 34
in a moment ɪn ə 'məʊmənt
 51
in advance ɪn əd'vɑːns 30
India 'ɪndɪə 25
Indian 'ɪndɪən 25
informal ɪn'fɔːməl 58
information ˌɪnfə'meɪʃən
 27, 54
innocent 'ɪnəsənt 32
instructor ɪn'strʌktə 59
intelligent ɪn'telɪdʒənt 56
interested in 'ɪntrəstɪd ɪn
 57
Internet 'ɪntənet 16, 23
interview 'ɪntəvjuː 33
Irish 'aɪrɪʃ 25
Is everything all right? ɪz
 'evriθɪŋ ɔːl raɪt 20
it doesn't matter ɪt dʌznt
 'mætə 9
it takes (+ time) ɪt teɪks 41
It's … here ɪts hɪə 16
It's a … day ɪts ə deɪ 26
it's up to you ɪts ʌp tə
 juː 9
Italian ɪ'tæliən 25
Italy 'ɪtəli 25
jacket 'dʒækɪt 4
January 'dʒænjuəri 50
Japan dʒə'pæn 25
jazz dʒæz 24
jeans dʒiːnz 4
job dʒɒb 14
journalist 'dʒɜːnəlɪst 33
journey 'dʒɜːni 30
judo 'dʒuːdəʊ 21
July dʒʊ'laɪ 50
jump dʒʌmp 47
jumper 'dʒʌmpə 4
June dʒuːn 50
karate kə'rɑːti 21
kayaking 'kaɪækɪŋ 21
key kiː 19
keyboard 'kiːbɔːd 16
kid kɪd 29
kilo 'kiːləʊ 54
kind kaɪnd 56
king kɪŋ 31
kitchen 'kɪtʃɪn 11
kitchen roll 'kɪtʃɪn rəʊl 11
knee niː 3

knife naɪf 11
lake leɪk 28
lamb læm 29
lamp læmp 13
land lænd 30
laptop 'læptɒp 16
last lɑːst 51
late for leɪt fə 34
law lɔː 32
leap year liːp jɪə 50
learn lɜːn 15, 24
leather 'leðə 29
leave liːv 30
left left 27, 52
leg leg 3
lend lend 60
let's lets 9
letter 'letə 16
letter box 'letə bɒks 16
letters 'letəz 16
librarian laɪ'breəriən 14
library 'laɪbrəri 27
lift lɪft 19
light laɪt 12, 13
light switch laɪt swɪtʃ 13
lightning 'laɪtnɪŋ 26
like laɪk 7, 21, 49
lion laɪən 29
lip lɪp 3
lipstick 'lɪpstɪk 3
listen (to) 'lɪsən 13, 23,
 24, 45
listen to 'lɪsən tə 57
litre 'liːtə 54
living room 'lɪvɪŋ ruːm 13
loaf ləʊf 54
local 'ləʊkəl 17
long lɒŋ 5
look after lʊk 'ɑːftə 57
look at lʊk æt 57
look for lʊk fɔː 27, 34, 57
look forward to lʊk 'fɔːwəd
 tə 57
look like lʊk laɪk 5
look out lʊk aʊt 9
loose luːs 60
lose luːz 34, 60
loud laʊd 53
loudly 'laʊdli 53
love lʌv 7, 22
lovely 'lʌvli 55, 56
luggage 'lʌgɪdʒ 17, 19, 30,
 54

magazine ˌmægə'ziːn 23,
 33
main course meɪn kɔːs 20
make meɪk 12
make a (phone) call meɪk ə
 kɔːl 16
make a choice meɪk ə
 tʃɔɪs 39
make a film meɪk ə
 fɪlm 39
make a mess meɪk ə
 mes 39
make a mistake meɪk ə
 mɪ'steɪk 39
make a noise meɪk ə
 nɔɪz 39
make a photocopy meɪk ə
 'fəʊtəˌkɒpi 39
make a video meɪk ə
 'vɪdiəʊ 39
make an appointment meɪk
 æn ə'pɔɪntmənt 39
make breakfast meɪk
 'brekfəst 39
make dinner meɪk 'dɪnə 39,
 45
make hot chocolate meɪk
 hɒt 'tʃɒklət 39
make lunch meɪk lʌnʃ 39
make me (feel) meɪk
 miː 39
make my bed meɪk maɪ
 bed 39
make some coffee meɪk səm
 'kɒfi 39
make some tea meɪk səm
 tiː 39
malaria mə'leəriə 6
man-made ˌmæn'meɪd 35
manner 'mænə 53
map mæp 30
March mɑːtʃ 50
marriage 'mærɪdʒ 2
married 'mærɪd 2
maths mæθs 15
May meɪ 50
meal miːl 20
meat miːt 10, 29
mechanic mɪ'kænɪk 14
media 'miːdiə 33
medium 'miːdiəm 5, 20
memory stick 'meməri
 stɪk 16

men's clothes menz
  kləʊðz 18
mend mend 34
menu 'menju: 20
Merry Christmas 'meri
  'krɪsməs 8, 46
message 'mesɪdʒ 16
microwave
  'maɪkrəweɪv 11
middle 'mɪdəl 52
middle-aged ˌmɪdəl'eɪdʒd 5
milk mɪlk 10, 29, 54
mineral water 'mɪnərəl
  'wɔːtə 10
mini-bar 'mɪni bɑː 19
minus 'maɪnəs 26
minute mɪnɪt 50
mirror 'mɪrə 12
miss mɪs 47
mixed mɪkst 20
mobile 'məʊbaɪl 16
mobile device 'məʊbaɪl
  dɪ'vaɪs 16
modern languages 'mɒdən
  'læŋgwɪdʒɪz 15
moment 'məʊmənt 51
Monday 'mʌndeɪ 50
money 'mʌni 17, 19, 54
monkey 'mʌŋki 29
month mʌnθ 50
mood muːd 34
morning 'mɔːnɪŋ 33, 50
Moroccan mə'rɒkən 25
Morocco mə'rɒkəʊ 25
mosquito mɒs'kiːtəʊ 6
mother 'mʌðə 1
motor racing 'məʊtə
  'reɪsɪŋ 21
motorbike 'məʊtəbaɪk 30
motorcycle 'məʊtəˌsaɪkəl
  30
mountain 'maʊntɪn 28
mouse maʊs 16
moustache mə'stɑːʃ 5
mouth maʊθ 3
move muːv 47
MP3 player empiː'θriː
  'pleɪə 23, 24
mug mʌg 11, 32
mugger 'mʌgə 32
mugging 'mʌgɪŋ 32
murder 'mɜːdə 32
murderer 'mɜːdərə 32
mushroom(s) 'mʌʃrʊm 10,
  20

music 'mjuːzɪk 15, 24
musical 'mjuːzɪkəl 22, 24
musical instruments
  'mjuːzɪkəl
  'ɪntstrəmənts 24
musician mjuː'zɪʃən 24
nail neɪl 3
national park 'næʃnəl pɑːk
  28
natural disaster 'nætʃrəl
  dɪ'zɑːstə 35
nature 'neɪtʃə 28, 33
naughty 'nɔːti 56
neck nek 3
negative 'negətɪv 56
nephew 'nefjuː 1
never 'nevə 51
new potato(es) njuː
  pə'teɪtəʊ 20
New Year's Day njuː jɪəz
  deɪ 31
New Year's Eve njuː jɪəz
  iːv 31
New Zealand ˌnjuː 'ziːlənd
  25
news njuːz 33, 54
newsagent('s) 'njuːzˌeɪdʒənt
  18
newspaper 'njuːsˌpeɪpə 23,
  33
next nekst 51
nice naɪs 55, 56
niece niːs 1
night naɪt 60
nightlife 'naɪtlaɪf 17
no smoking nəʊ 'sməʊkɪŋ
  27
non-smoking nɒn 'sməʊkɪŋ
  58
normally 'nɔːməli 12, 45
nose nəʊz 3
not too bad nɒt tuː bæd 8
note nəʊt 18
notebook 'nəʊtbʊk 15
nothing 'nʌθɪŋ 23
noticeboard 'nəʊtɪsbɔːd
  15
noun naʊn 48
novel 'nɒvəl 23
November nə'vembə 50
now naʊ 51
now and then naʊ ənd ðen
  51
number 'nʌmbə 27
nurse nɜːs 14

nursery school 'nɜːsri
  skuːl 31
o'clock əʊ'klɒk 51
occasionally ə'keɪʒənli 51
October ɒk'təʊbə 50
office 'ɒfɪs 14
often 'ɒfən 51
Oh dear əʊ dɪə 9
OHP (overhead projector)
  əʊeɪtʃ'piː 15
old əʊld 5
on ɒn 52
on strike ɒn straɪk 35
on the left ɒn ðə left 52
on the right ɒn ðə raɪt 52
once wʌns 51
onion 'ʌnjən 10
online ˌɒn'laɪn 16, 23, 33
online check-in ˌɒn'laɪn tʃek
  ɪn 30
only 'əʊnli 49
only child 'əʊnli tʃaɪld 1
open 'əʊpən 18
opera 'ɒpərə 24
or ɔː 49
orange 'ɒrɪndʒ 10
orchestra 'ɔːkɪstrə 24
order 'ɔːdə 20
out aʊt 52
out of order aʊt əv 'ɔːdə
  27, 34
outside line ˌaʊt'saɪd laɪn
  19
oven 'ʌvən 31
over there 'əʊvə ðeə 19
overweight 'əʊvəweɪt 5
package holiday 'pækɪdʒ
  'hɒlədeɪ 17
pain peɪn 3
pair of trousers / shorts /
  glasses peər əv 'traʊzəz /
  ʃɔːts / 'glɑːsɪz 4
Pakistan ˌpɑːkɪ'stɑːn 25
Pakistani ˌpɑːkɪ'stɑːni 25
paper 'peɪpə 33
paragraph 'pærəgrɑːf 48
parents 'peərənts 1
park pɑːk 27
parrot 'pærət 29
pass pɑːs 13, 47
pass an exam pɑːs ən
  ɪg'zæm 15
passport 'pɑːspɔːt 17, 30
past pɑːst 51

take ... for a walk teɪk fɔːr
ə wɔːk 29
take ... off teɪk ɒf 4
take a course teɪk ə kɔːs
41
take a message teɪk ə
'mesɪdʒ 16
take a photo teɪk ə 'fəʊtəʊ
41
take a taxi teɪk ə 'tæksi 41
take an exam teɪk ən
ɪg'zæm 15, 41
take drugs teɪk drʌgz 32
take off teɪk ɒf 30, 44
take the bus teɪk ðə bʌs
41
take the train teɪk ðə treɪn
41
take the underground teɪk
ðə 'ʌndəgraʊnd 41
take-away teɪk ə'weɪ 20
talk tɔːk 23, 46
talk show tɔːk ʃəʊ 33
tall tɔːl 5
tap tæp 11
tape recorder teɪp rɪ'kɔːdə
15
taxi 'tæksi 30, 41
taxi driver 'tæksi 'draɪvə
14
tea tiː 10, 36, 54
tea towel tiː taʊəl 11
teach tiːtʃ 15
teacher 'tiːtʃə 14, 15
teapot 'tiːpɒt 11
teenage 'tiːneɪdʒ 33
teeth tiːθ 3
telephone (phone) 'telɪfəʊn
12, 16
television (TV) 'telɪvɪʒən
12, 13
tell (someone) a joke tel ə
dʒəʊk 46
tell (someone) a story tel ə
'stɔːri 46
tell (someone) the time tel
ðə taɪm 46
tell someone your address
tel 'sʌmwʌn jɔːr ə'dres 46
tell someone your name tel
'sʌmwʌn jɔː neɪm 46
tell someone your phone
number tel 'sʌmwʌn jɔː
fəʊn 'nʌmbə 46

tennis 'tenɪs 21
terrible 'terəbəl 55
terrorism 'terərɪzəm 32
terrorist 'terərɪst 32
text tekst 16
textbook 'teksbʊk 15
Thai taɪ 25
Thailand 'taɪlænd 25
than ðæn 49
thank for θæŋk fɔː 57
thank you θæŋk juː 8, 46
thanks θæŋks 8
then ðen 51
there ðeə 52
thin θɪn 5
think about θɪŋk ə'baʊt 57
third θɜːd 18
thirsty 'θɜːsti 7
thriller 'θrɪlə 22
thumb θʌm 3
thunder 'θʌndə 26, 26
thunderstorm 'θʌndəstɔːm
26
thundery 'θʌndəri 26
Thursday 'θɜːzdeɪ 50
ticket 'tɪkɪt 30
tidy 'taɪdi 34
tie taɪ 4
tiger 'taɪgə 29
tights taɪts 4
timetable 'taɪm,teɪbəl 30
(four) times a month taɪmz
ə mʌnθ 51
(three) times a week taɪmz ə
wiːk 45
tired taɪəd 7
today tə'deɪ 50, 51
toe təʊ 3
toilet 'tɔɪlət 12
tomato(es) tə'mɑːtəʊ 10
tomorrow tə'mɒrəʊ 50,
51
too tuː 49
too much tuː mʌtʃ 34
tooth tuːθ 3
toothache 'tuːθeɪk 6
toothbrush 'tuːθbrʌʃ 12
toothpaste 'tuːθpeɪst 12
top tɒp 52
tortoise 'tɔːtəs 29
tourist (information)
office 'tʊərɪst 'ɒfɪs 27
towel taʊəl 12
town taʊn 27, 28
town hall taʊn hɔːl 27

toys tɔɪz 18
traffic 'træfɪk 54
traffic jam 'træfɪk dʒæm
35
traffic warden 'træfɪk
'wɔːdən 14
train treɪn 14, 17, 27, 30
trainers 'treɪnəz 4
train station treɪn 'steɪʃən
27
transport 'trænspɔːt 47
travel 'trævəl 54
traveller's cheques 'trævələz
tʃeks 17
travelling 'trævəlɪŋ 30
tropical 'trɒpɪkəl 6
trousers 'traʊzəz 4
trumpet 'trʌmpɪt 24
trumpet-player 'trʌmpɪt
'pleɪə 24
try on traɪ ɒn 18
T-shirt 'tiːʃɜːt 4
Tuesday 'tjuːzdeɪ 50
Tunisia tjuː'nɪziə 25
Tunisian tjuː'nɪziən 25
turn tɜːn 27
turn down tɜːn daʊn 44
turn off tɜːn ɒf 12, 13, 44
turn on tɜːn ɒn 13, 44
turn up tɜːn ʌp 44
TV ,tiː'viː 13, 19, 22, 23,
33
twice twaɪs 51
ugly 'ʌgli 5
UK ,juː'keɪ 25
umbrella ʌm'brelə 4
uncle 'ʌŋkəl 1
uncountable ʌn'kaʊntəbəl
54
underground 'ʌndəgraʊnd
30
unemployed ,ʌnɪm'plɔɪd
35
unfriendly ʌn'frendli 53
unhappy ʌn'hæpi 56, 58
United States (the US)
juː,naɪtɪd'steɪts 25
university ,juːnɪ'vɜːsəti 15
unsafe ʌn'seɪf 58
untidy ʌn'taɪdi 34
upset ʌp'set 7
upstairs ʌp'steəz 12
USA ,juːes'eɪ 25
useful 'juːsfəl 59
useless 'juːsləs 59

usually 'juːʒəli 45, 51

Valentine's Day 'væləntaɪnz deɪ 31

vandal 'vændəl 32

vandalism 'vændəlɪzəm 32

vegetable(s) 'vedʒtəbəl 10, 20

vegetarian ˌvedʒɪ'teəriən 10

verb vɜːb 48

very 'veri 55

village 'vɪlɪdʒ 28

violin ˌvaɪə'lɪn 24

violinist vaɪə'lɪnɪst 24

visa 'viːzə 17

voicemail 'vɔɪsmeɪl 16

volleyball 'vɒlibɔːl 21

waist weɪst 3

wait for weɪt fɔː 57, 60

waiter 'weɪtə 14

wake up weɪk ʌp 12, 45

wake-up call weɪk ʌp kɔːl 19

walk wɔːk 28, 47

walking holiday 'wɔːkɪŋ 'hɒlədeɪ 17

want wɒnt 7

war wɔː 35

wardrobe 'wɔːdrəʊb 12

wash wɒʃ 3

wash clothes wɒʃ kləʊðz 45

washing machine 'wɒʃɪŋ mə'ʃiːn 11

washing-up liquid 'wɒʃɪŋ ʌp 'lɪkwɪd 11

watch wɒtʃ 4, 13, 22, 23, 33, 45

water 'wɔːtə 29, 34, 54

way weɪ 53

wear weə 4

weather 'weðə 26, 54

wedding 'wedɪŋ 2

Wednesday 'wenzdeɪ 50

week wiːk 50

weekend ˌwiːk'end 50

weigh weɪ 2, 5

weight weɪt 5

well wel 6, 7, 53

well done wel dʌn 8, 9

well-behaved ˌwelbɪ'heɪvd 56

well-done ˌwel'dʌn 20

western 'westən 22

wet wet 26

what a pity wɒt ə 'pɪti 9

What about …? wɒt ə'baʊt 9

What time do you ….? wɒt taɪm də ju 45

What's his/her job? wɒts hɪz/hɜː dʒɒb 14

What's on …? wɒts ɒn 22

What's on TV? wɒts ɒn ˌtiː'viː 33

What's the weather like? wɒts ðə 'weðə laɪk 26

What's your favourite …? wɒts jɔː 'feɪvərɪt 21

when wen 49

Where can I find …? weə kən aɪ faɪnd 11

Where does … go? weə dəz gəʊ 11

Where is …? weər ɪz 27

Why don't …? waɪ dəʊnt 9

widowed 'wɪdəʊd 2

wife waɪf 1

wild animal waɪld 'ænɪməl 29

wildlife 'waɪldlaɪf 28

wind wɪnd 26

window 'wɪndəʊ 13

windy 'wɪndi 26

wine waɪn 10

wine list waɪn lɪst 20

winter 'wɪntə 50

winter holiday 'wɪntə 'hɒlədeɪ 17

women's wear wɪmɪnz weə 18

wonderful 'wʌndəfəl 55, 56

wood wʊd 28

wool wʊl 29

work wɜːk 14, 34, 54

worker 'wɜːkə 59

worktop 'wɜːktɒp 11

Would you like …? wʊd ju laɪk 20

write raɪt 15

write emails raɪt iːmeɪlz 45

write letters raɪt 'letəz 45

wrong rɒŋ 53

year jɪə 50, 51

yesterday 'jestədeɪ 50

Yorkshire pudding 'jɔːkʃə 'pʊdɪŋ 31

young jʌŋ 5

zoo zuː 29

Irregular verbs

Most verbs in English are regular but some of the most common verbs in English are irregular. The forms here are the infinitive (*go, come*), the past simple (*went, came*) and the past participle (*gone, come*).

A All forms the same

cost	cost	cost
cut /kʌt/	cut	cut
hurt	hurt	hurt
let	let	let
put /pʊt/	put	put
shut /ʃʌt/	shut	shut

B Two different forms

beat	beat	beaten
become	became	become
bring	brought	brought
buy	bought	bought
catch	caught	caught
come	came	come
feel	felt	felt
fight	fought	fought
find	found	found
get	got	got
have	had	had
hear	heard	heard
keep	kept	kept
leave	left	left
learn	learnt	learnt
lose	lost	lost
make	made	made
meet	met	met
pay	paid /peɪd/	paid
read /riːd/	read /red/	read /red/
run	ran	run
say	said /sed/	said
sell	sold	sold
shine	shone	shone
shoot	shot	shot
sit	sat	sat
sleep	slept	slept
spend	spent	spent
stand	stood	stood
teach	taught	taught
tell	told	told
think	thought	thought
win	won	won
understand	understood	understood

C Three different forms

be	was / were	been
begin	began	begun
break	broke	broken
choose	chose	chosen
do	did	done
drink	drank	drunk
drive	drove	driven
eat	ate	eaten
fall	fell	fallen
fly	flew	flown
forget	forgot	forgotten
give	gave	given
go	went	gone
know	knew	known
ride	rode	ridden
rise	rose	risen
sing	sang	sung
speak	spoke	spoken
steal	stole	stolen
swim	swam	swum
take	took	taken
throw	threw	thrown
wake	woke	woken
wear	wore	worn
write	wrote	written

Tip

When you learn a new irregular verb, add it to one of the groups of verbs on these pages.

How to learn vocabulary

To learn a lot of vocabulary, you have to do different things.

1 Study each unit of the book carefully and do all the exercises. Check your answers with your teacher. Repeat the units after a month, and then again after three months, and see how much you have learnt and how much you have forgotten. Repeating work is very important.

2 Keep a vocabulary notebook. Students who regularly make notes in a separate notebook often do better in tests and examinations than students who do not keep a notebook.

3 Use different ways of recording things in your notebook. For example, every time you see or hear an interesting phrase, write it in your notebook, and write who said it or wrote it, and in what situation, as well as what it means. Here are some examples:

ready: *(person at the door of a theatre, to all the people waiting)* 'Have your tickets ready, please!' = have your ticket in your hand

else: *(person in a restaurant)* 'Would you like anything else?' = more or in addition or different

rush hour: *(person who is about to leave home for work)* 'I'm going early so that I miss the rush hour' = the times when there are lots of people travelling to work in the morning or when people are travelling home in the evening

Making notes of the situations words are used in will help you to remember them and to use them at the right moment.

4 Use diagrams and other visual aids to help you learn and remember words and phrases. Word bubbles are very easy to draw and can help you remember the different meanings and uses of words. Here is an example for the word *play*, which can be a verb or a noun:

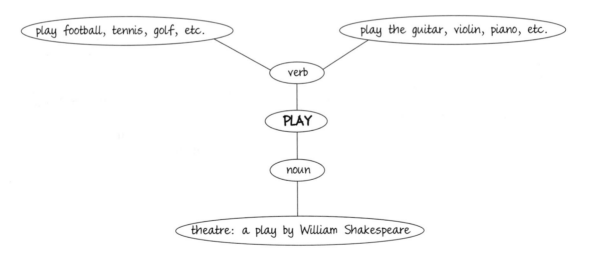

Charts can also help you to organise information about words. This student has made notes in her vocabulary notebook about useful verbs and the nouns we use them with:

take	a taxi a message violin lessons	catch	a cold a criminal a ball	make	dinner a mistake an appointment	do	my homework somebody a favour my best (to)

How to use the *English Vocabulary in Use Elementary* CD-ROM to learn vocabulary

Your copy of *English Vocabulary in Use Elementary* comes with a CD-ROM. You can use the CD-ROM to improve your English vocabulary. These two pages answer some common questions about the CD-ROM.

What is on the CD-ROM?

The CD-ROM contains:

- two practice activities for each unit of the book (120 in total)
- two vocabulary games, *Word Challenger* and *Falling Letters*
- a test maker
- a record and play-back function
- a dictionary function.

When should I use the CD-ROM?

You can use the CD-ROM before or after you do a unit in the book. This section will give you some suggestions.

Using the CD-ROM before you look at a unit in the book

The CD-ROM can help you discover how much vocabulary you already know about a topic. Try this:

- Choose a topic from the *Exercises* menu, for example *Food and drink* in the *At home* section.
- Complete the two exercises. After each exercise, click *Check your answers* to see how many questions you got right. Make a note of any words you found difficult.
- Now go to the relevant unit of the book. Study the notes on the left-hand page. Try to find the words you didn't know from the CD-ROM. Complete the exercises on the right-hand page.
- Finally, return to the CD-ROM. Look at the *My progress* section. Can you improve your score this time? Complete the two exercises again for the same unit.

Using the CD-ROM after you look at a unit in the book

The CD-ROM can help you to remember words you learnt from the book. This kind of revision is very important if you want to remember vocabulary. Try this:

- When you complete a unit from the book, write the date at the top of the page.
- One week later, go to the CD-ROM and do the two exercises from that unit. How much vocabulary can you remember? Make a note of any words you found difficult or couldn't remember.
- Go back to the unit in the book and look for the words you didn't know. Study the words again.
- Finally, return to the CD-ROM and complete the two exercises again. Did you remember those difficult words?

The CD-ROM can also help you test yourself. You can even personalise the tests to cover the topics that *you* want to practise. Try this:

- When you finish a group of units in the book (for example, the nine units in the *People* section), go to the CD-ROM and make a test on the vocabulary from those units. The CD-ROM will create five test questions from each of those units. For an extra challenge, use the time limit function. If your score is low, look at the units again. Then create a new test and try to improve your score.
- Alternatively, create a test when you have completed the whole book. Choose units at random or concentrate on units that you found difficult.

Can the CD-ROM help me with my pronunciation?

Yes, it can. The CD-ROM has a record and play-back function which you can use to practise your pronunciation. Try this:

- When you have completed an exercise on the CD-ROM, click the green arrow to hear a model pronunciation of the words or sentences.
- Then click the red *Record your voice* button at the bottom of the screen. Practise saying the word or sentence.
- Now click the green *Play your voice* arrow at the bottom of the screen. Does your pronunciation sound correct? Listen to the model pronunciation again to check.
- Record your voice again if necessary.

Can I use the CD-ROM for fun?

Yes, of course! We hope you will find all of the exercises fun. However, there are also two games which can help you to practise vocabulary in a fun way.

- In *Word Challenger*, you score points by choosing the correct word for the picture. This game can help you to remember what words mean. You can make the game easier or harder by using the different options. If you write down your score after each game, you can try to improve it next time.
- In *Falling Letters*, you can practise listening and spelling. Try to score as many points as you can in the time available. Write down your score and try to improve it next time.

Both these games are quick and fun. Just playing for five or ten minutes a day can help you to remember more vocabulary. And to make things even more fun, you can have a competition with a friend. Who can score the most points?

What else can the CD-ROM do?

Remember that the CD-ROM also has a dictionary function. You can use it to look up any words that you don't know. You will need an internet connection for this.

Also remember that you can check your progress at any time using the *Progress* section. This will help you to see which exercises you have completed. It can also show you areas where you need more practice. In those cases, go back to the book and study the left-hand pages again.

We hope you enjoy using the *English Vocabulary in Use Elementary* CD-ROM.

Also available:

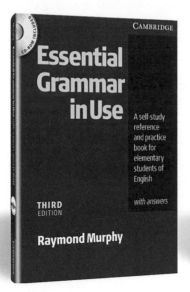

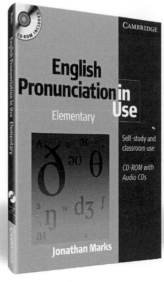

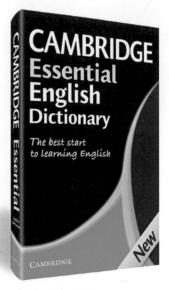

978-0-521-67543-7   978-0-521-69373-8   978-0-521-00537-1